Born to be Rich

by Janine A. Ingram

Born to be Rich, LLC
Chicago, Illinois

Born to be Rich, LLC
773-447-5591
www.borntoberich.org

ISBN-13: 978-0-615-34134-7
LCCN: 2009913477

Cover design: Barron Steward of www.barronsteward.com
Editorial Team: Lissa Woodson, Patricia Boer, Erica Weber
Interior Book Design: Lissa Woodson of www.macrompg.com

Distributed by Ingram Book Group

Born to be Rich, LLC trade paperback edition April 2010

10   9   8   7   6   5   4   3   2   1
Manufactured and Printed in the United States of America

For information regarding discounts for bulk purchases, please contact us at 773-447-5591.

Acknowledgments

I want to give thanks to the ALMIGHTY CREATOR, GOD, the GREAT I AM THAT I AM. The Universe is amazing. I am truly grateful for being on this earth scene at this time. I am in such gratitude to be used as a vessel to express my creativity. Living in the light and the spirit of joy is life most precious gift.

I give thanks for my Angels: Ganesh for keeping my path smooth, Gabriel for opening my creative channels, Michael for protection, Lakshmi for teaching me how to receive, Pele for the gift of passion, and Abundantia for reminding me we live in a lavish universe with overflow and abundance awaiting our awakening.

I am thankful for my beautiful mother, Anastasia McAdoo, who is growing everyday to become exactly what God created her to be. I thank God for using you as the vehicle to bring me to the earth.

Thank you for my wonderful sisters; Jessie Purnell I appreciate you for being the rock of the family who taught integrity and truth as well as lived it; Del Billups the middle sister (LOL), I appreciate your beauty and style; our joy of sharing music. Thank you for your energy.

My nephew, Gerard Purnell, where would I be without your love? We grew up like brothers and sisters and I love you.

Brenton, I appreciate you for always supporting my dreams, even when the risk jeopardized the family. Thank you for being a phenomenal dad; my best friend still, today.

I am grateful for my three amazing girls: Diamond, I thank God everyday for your love. You are the best. Ebony, my artist, thank you for being so creative, reminding me how beautiful life can be. I am so very proud of you. Asia, my scientist, I appreciate you and how you have the courage to live your dreams regardless of anyone's opinions. You girls are the reason I live. You all bring me so much joy, I can't imagine life without you. I am excited about the women you all are becoming. The world better watch out, the Ingram girls are on the earth scene. The world is your stage—work it!!!!

My bonus children: Brenton, Chris, Justin, and Devon. My Bonus Nieces and Nephews: Brandy, Brandon, Arthur, Robbie, Marrisa, Revon, Shawn, Terrie and Maurice--I appreciate you all for bringing color to my life.

Myra Neal, for always being there and giving great words of wisdom. Thank you for keeping me up through this process. Where would this book be without you?

Sherrion Neal thanks for assisting me. I'm still waiting on you to create that book that is inside of you.

Rochelle Knox, I am grateful for your belief in me, always being there and giving me so much joy and love. Thank you for making me a part of your family. Thank you for another Grandmother that my children can depend on for support in so many ways. My whole family loves you so very much. We appreciate you.

Darrell Knox, I appreciate you for you being you.

My brother-in-laws, Robert and Willie, for always being there. You are so appreciated. Thank you.

Nicole Jones, for being my friend. Girl you are the bomb!! Words cannot express the joy my heart has for you. I truly appreciate you for your love, encouragement, and faith. I am grateful God sent me in your path. I thank you for seeing in me what I could not see in myself. Thank you for pushing me. Keep letting God use you as a vessel. He has a mighty work in store for you.

Tiffany Hill, thank you for your joy and love. Thank you for Teri and Taji, between you and your husband Terry, you are doing a wonderful job, you have created a phenomenal family. I am so very proud of the Hill family. God is using you to remind us what a strong family can bring to a community.

Lissa Woodson (Naleighna Kai), I am grateful for God sending you my way. I have grown tremendously since our first meeting. Thank you for assisting me in the birthing process of this book. You have a true passion for bringing words to print. I know life is about to bring all your dreams to fruition. See you at the top! Patricia Boer and Erica Weber—Thank you.

Jeremy "J.L." Woodson of www.macrompg.com, I appreciate my beautiful website. Your creativity leaves me speechless. I thank God for you. I pray that your book and your mother's books shoot straight to the top.

Renae Baines, I thank you for our friendship over the years. Adrienne Bennett, you are the best!

Jacqueline Davis, and Michael Davis, the son we share, for the love and support. Ms. Nancy Roddy, thank you for your words of wisdom over the years.

Louanne Fries, for always being inspiring. You always said there was a book inside of me.

Thomas Cole and Matthew Gambs of Diamond Bank; Mirion Green, Ricky O'Neal, Mr. & Mrs. Versia and Albert Green, and Mark Haygood. Thank you!

My Intenders family: Sesvalah, Tehuti, and Debra.

Barron Steward of www.barronsteward.com for the cover design. You are such an amazing artist.

I thank my Prayer line family. Your support and love keeps me living in Faith.

I thank everyone who is, or has been a part my life and helped to shape the very essence of who I am today. So if I have not mentioned your name, know that you are a blessing to me and for that I am Grateful.

Thank You

Thank you for purchasing my book. You have attracted this book for a reason. It is my hope this information does for you what it has done for me: provide the tools and guidance to become a prosperous person holistically.

I thank my Father in Heaven for transforming me inside and out on this journey to manifesting true wealth. More importantly, I thank Him for the person I have become spiritually and for understanding how to use MY spiritual tools every day of my life. As I become a spiritual architect, building my life with bricks of courage, faith, integrity and love, I now know that my life is not about me but instead about each life that I touch.

Again, thank you, and I hope you enjoy reading Born to be Rich!

Why Would I Write a Book Entitled, Born to be Rich?

There are many books out today that speak on the subject of prosperity, abundance, living your dreams and so much more. Information on these ideals is coming from all areas of the globe and, if we're receptive, it's coming from all points of the Universe. We are all teachers and students; we all have something to give. It was through the process of learning how to love, forgive and manifest my own abundance that the Universe began to use me, a woman who has always been guided and protected by the Creator, as a channel to show others how it could be done. This book serves to remind you that you were born to live an extraordinary life and have fulfillment in every area of that life.

How many times have we heard, "we are created in the image and likeness of God?" I know that this is a statement that people use repeatedly, but it is a powerful message, especially when one understands its true meaning. Being created in the image and likeness of God is more than a reference to our beautiful physical beings. It is about the spirit that resides in us, that animates our bodies. The spirit that lives, observes, experiences life in all its wondrous, challenging, and rewarding forms. And if that spirit is an image and likeness of an original, powerful, creative being, then you have the power to create the world you desire. That single thought is incredible!

We can accomplish anything through the strength of Christ. I'm speaking of that Christ Consciousness that was displayed by the Master Teacher who turned water into wine, healed the sick, fed the multitudes and performed miracles that astounded those around him then, and those who are studying him today.

My prayer for everyone who reads this book is that it helps bring health, supernatural favor, love, joy and abundance as well as an overflow of peace into your lives. It is my hope that this book inspires, uplifts and restores your "in it to win it" attitude! Remember to dream those God-sized dreams! Follow me through the journey and learn what it means when you are …Born to Be Rich.

So let the God times roll!

What Does It Mean to Be Rich?

Rich, as defined by Webster, means possessing or controlling great wealth; wealthy; valuable; abundant. Being truly rich means leading a fulfilling life. Holistically it means extraordinary success, or living with a purpose in every key area of your life including:

- Spiritual
- Relationships
- Health
- Career
- Finance
- Love
- Joy

So often there is a misconception of success, of what being rich or wealthy actually means. Most define wealth by their material possessions or by how much money they can accumulate. But wealth is truly measured by the degree that you are experiencing peace, love, joy, health, and abundance in your world. The Bible is filled with succulent promises regarding prosperity; we are supposed to be prosperous. It is our Divine right to be rich. Even in America our money's motto is "IN GOD WE TRUST." The Universe is friendly to our desires, and it was the Almighty Creator, of course, who designed it that way.

In my research of the word "prosperity" I found what makes the great, well great. The secret to true wealth is being in alignment with the purpose for which you were created. You see, purpose gave life to you. You did not give life to your purpose.

Deuteronomy 8:18 states: "But thou shall remember Jehovah thy God, for it is He that giveth thee power to get wealth."

Make a decision to choose faith over fear. Trust in spiritual laws that were designed to govern every aspect of your life. Your part is to be a good receiver, prepare for your blessings and rejoice with an attitude of gratitude. As you live the life you were born to live, remember to open yourself to the abundance that is available to you in a never-ending supply. Be a blessing to others and reap the rich rewards of living your Divine purpose. Your life is calling you toward all that you were born to be.

Are you ready?

The Beginning of the Beginning

My first spark of consciousness on the journey to becoming rich happened at age twelve. It was like any other day for me except I had stayed home from school because I wasn't feeling very well. Having to work, my Mom sent me to my sister's house for the day. I was fascinated with the books she always kept handy and would read them every opportunity I could between my studies. Books have always excited me and whenever I had the occasion, I could be found with a book in my hands. Once there, I snuggled into a spot near her bookshelf, and looked up to scan the rows of books. For some reason, *Think and Grow Rich* by Napoleon Hill seemed to shout out at me. This wasn't light material for a twelve-year old, but the title drew me in. I picked it up and started reading.

The most interesting thing about that book was that it made me realize that I could actually control my own life. This was an amazing concept because I always knew there was something more to life; that there was a power beyond what I actually understood. This epiphany brought to mind an incident that had happened two years earlier. One night I dreamt that I took a test, one harder than we had ever been given before, and I scored 100 percent on it. The next day, I arrived at school and learned about an exam scheduled for that afternoon. I don't remember studying or preparing for it, but I do remember that when I received the results from the test there was a big red

100 at the top! Even then, seeing things in my dreams come to pass was the first inclination I had of a mind-manifestation connection. Reading Think and Grow Rich was my first "Ah ha" moment, and the second step in understanding how to manifest my desires in life.

I started working out the principles of abundance and prosperity at age twelve, writing my goals and dreams down on paper. Soon after I began doing this, I recognized the things I wrote down began to happen. Certain classes I had wanted to take were suddenly open where they hadn't been beforehand. Certain trips I desired to experience were available to me even though my mother didn't have the funds to pay for them. The biggest manifestation was the opportunity to be reunited with my mother once again. At that time in my life, due to circumstances beyond my control, I was separated from her. But like most children who do not understand the workings of adults and their decisions, I longed to be with her. These principles did not fail me even then as I wrote that request on a sheet of paper as one of my goals. Despite whatever obstacles were presented, I was finally allowed to go and live with my mother for three years.

At age fifteen I joined Johnnie Coleman's Church, Christ Universal Temple (CUT)—a non-denominational church founded on New Thought and The Science of Mind philosophies. It was in this place of worship that I learned similar principles as those taught in Think and Grow Rich. The only difference was that these principles had a Biblical foundation. The new principles I was taught were examples of what it means to bring spiritual law into manifestation and realize your desires. So I gravitated from excelling in classes, to taking class trips, to high fashion clothes and becoming a model. Well, I did manage to land a ten-page spread in After Five magazine and I had a love affair with stylish clothes and shoes. Then at a later time, I wanted to date a certain guy and wrote him on the list, too. When I was walking down the street not too long afterward, he took a pointed interest in me and we ended up dating for a while. He treated me like a princess, and even bought my graduation dress as well as other wonderful things from the money he made at his little job.

At Christ Universal Temple (CUT) I was introduced to Catherine Ponder, the woman who would change my life forever. She taught me why and how we affirm things in our life through the spoken word. She was a petite, white-haired woman whose voice did not resonate the same as the bold Johnnie Coleman, but whose writing and words were equally as profound; both had their own strength and influence. Through Catherine Ponder I learned about dream-building, treasure-mapping (also known as vision boards) and discovered why each person should have a master plan for his or her life. All of that was wonderful, but it was the compilation of stories from the Bible in her millionaire series that truly illustrated points of prosperity that spoke to my soul like nothing ever had before.

I grew up in a sanctified church with very strong principles of what was right and what was wrong, with no gray area in between. It wasn't uncommon to be in the temple from, as the Southerners called it, "can't see" to "can't see." Because of the strict rules, I swore up and down that I would not go to church when I became an adult. I only kept that vow for about five years. No matter how hard I tried, I couldn't forget the stories and the teachings from that church. They were deeply rooted in me and were part of who I was as a person. When I finally read the Millionaires of Genesis, Millionaire Joshua, Millionaire

Moses and the Millionaire from Nazareth, combined with the principles described in Think and Grow Rich and what was taught at CUT, the pieces came together and the answers became crystal clear.

One thing was for certain, no matter what my meager beginnings were, I was born to be rich. Each of the men in the millionaire series started with nothing but on their path they came into prosperity as life progressed. Not only were their physical desires fulfilled, but they also developed a strong spiritual connection to the Creator that was like a gateway to Heaven. Take Jesus, for example. Jesus was the Master Teacher and people took care of him wherever he traveled. He lacked for nothing, wore the finest of clothes which, today, might translate into Armani, Versace and other specialty designers. It goes without saying that with the ability to turn five loaves of bread and two fish into enough food to feed 5,000 hungry souls, he himself would never go hungry. Not to mention he could turn water into wine, so I'm certain he was invited to all the best parties. Jesus did indeed have a modest beginning, having been born in secrecy, and his life shrouded in even more mystery. During his time on Earth, Jesus taught us that anyone who can achieve a spiritual connection will overcome any obstacle life has to offer.

As I started to understand that there was a different path for me, I felt like Moses, a man who was commissioned to do an awesome task that most would shy away from. God commanded him to speak to the Pharaoh and immediately Moses was like, "Who me?" I'm sure he looked around to see if there was someone behind him before saying, "Are you sure you have the right person? Maybe you mean my brother, Aaron. He's better-spoken than I am. You do know I stutter, right?"

Well, God knew exactly who he wanted for the job. Moses was preordained and had even survived a mass killing in a miraculous way that put him into the protection of the very person who sought to kill him. He grew up among the Egyptians and learned the mysteries of life. Later he would lead the charge to free the people who had been enslaved for centuries. Then he would go on to be a millionaire in his own right.

Joshua, who led the Israelites into the Promised Land a mere three days after taking leadership, was one of the twelve spies that Moses had sent into Canaan to check things out. The other ten spies he had sent came back and said, "Oh, no. There are giants over there. We can't go there. No siree! Not for us." However, Joshua and Caleb had a different take on things. "We can take 'em right now! Let's do it!" I can imagine them shifting from side to side, anxious to get moving.

Moses didn't share Joshua's excitement. Instead he had the wisdom to know that a plan was needed before action could be taken. Unfortunately, Moses didn't lead the people into the Promise Land because he was disobedient. God told him to speak to the mountain to get water to come out to quench their thirst. The children of Israel had been murmuring and complaining about it, so the first time God told Moses to strike the rock and water came. This time they were complaining again, which probably took Moses off his square, and in place of speaking to the rock as God commanded, he struck it instead. It might have eased his anger and fulfilled their immediate needs, but it cost him plenty. Even though he never made it to the Promised Land, he was still given everything he had been promised and those things he hadn't thought enough about to ask.

There was a time when I hadn't made the spiritual connection between manifesting and true healing. I could, and most times did, bring forth anything material that I desired, but I found that I still felt a void in my life. That void was emotional healing that needed to take place in order for me to feel truly fulfilled. I made the mistake of focusing on what I desired rather than on what I needed most—I needed healing from things that happened during my childhood.

At the point in my life when my mother was unable to care for me, I ended up in the homes of several different people. I could lie and say that some of them were good places, but the truth was that every place had a dangerous issue. One house was so infested that I refused to take off my clothes. I slept in my coat, was too scared to use a toothbrush and I certainly didn't dare eat any food in that place. Finally, my mother came and got me only to leave me at another home where I went to church every single day of the week. Though this place didn't have problems with four-legged visitors, it was the one place where my personal safety was threatened. This time sleeping with my clothes on was not to ward off critters smaller than my thumb; it was, as I thought of it, to protect me from the animals of the two-legged variety.

It felt like an eternity, but eventually I ended up once again at my mother's home. It was just the two of us, and it was great at least for a while. The summer between my eighth grade and freshman year of school she started a new relationship. This meant that I was left to fend for myself for a three-month period. Sometimes, when my mother was into someone or something new, nothing else seemed to matter; especially not the daughter she hadn't wanted in the first place. So there I was in a house, all alone, with no adult supervision. Most importantly, though, this also meant that there was no food to eat. As with most children, I learned to survive the best way I could in such dire circumstances. With everything I had been through as a child, I certainly knew how to take care of myself by this point.

A grocery store just up the street served as a convenient place to fill my belly and quiet my hunger. Unfortunately, most of the time, I had no money to pay for the food I needed. One day I was caught by the store's general manager—I'll never forget him. I had stashed a quart of milk, a German chocolate cake and a plum in my jacket. He pulled me aside, but instead of calling the police, he simply said, "Children don't just steal food unless they're hungry." He was right, of course. Children who stole for fun took candy, chips or toys. I, on the other hand, would come in for lightweight groceries; for something to fill my stomach for the time being or at least until another meal came along. The general manager told me to come to the store every Monday to get a bag of groceries, and for the three months during that summer I spent alone, I did exactly that.

This arrangement worked out well until the day my mother came home and said we were moving in with her new love interest. I didn't want to leave and cried my heart out; I begged to remain in that home. This place had always been a comfort for me. Even though I may have been lonely, I always had shelter, clothes and a place to get food. I had a feeling that because her interest wasn't with that place any longer, neither was her pocketbook. Regardless of my little set up, it was time to go by choice before we were forced to leave.

Moving into the next place proved more difficult than either of us imagined. Thankfully my sister came and rescued me from a precarious situation that resulted from of a disagreement with a relative of my mother's new friend. I had mistakenly taken a glass of vodka for water and emptied it to finish washing the dishes. The woman took high exception to my mistake and it earned me a few scrapes and bruises. With a single phone call from my perceptive nephew explaining the situation, my sister came for me right away. Fortunately, my mother was out of the city with her lover at the time, or I'm certain things would have been handled quite differently.

I prayed my way through every rough situation, and I knew God had my back. Even as I moved from one home to another, experiencing danger and fear instead of safety and love, I knew God was there to protect me. He answered my prayers when my sister opened her home to me, allowing me, for once in my life, to live in relative peace and tranquility, something I didn't know could even exist.

Staying with my sister was the best thing that could have ever happened to me. But here is where things got interesting; I had finally arrived at a place where someone loved and cared for me and had given me something no one else ever had. What did I give her in return? Rebellion. I seemed ungrateful, but the truth was that I didn't know how to accept love.

During my sophomore year of high school, because I had lived according to my own rules for so long, I wasn't used to living with structure and constraints set forth by someone else. There was never a curfew that I managed to make, and I can truly say that love brought my sister through it. It was prayer that kept me protected—because I will be honest here—I did some pretty crazy things.

I learned a lot from my sister's steadfast love. She is filled with integrity. It wasn't until much later in my life that her words would resonate within me—words about living a life of integrity, words about loving God, finding favor, living in purpose. Words that spoke to the essence of who she was.

My sister is a God-loving, warm-hearted, no-nonsense woman and she loved me. I mean, she truly loved me. I couldn't fathom that. What was love, anyway? That emotion was foreign to me at the time, and I certainly tested her on several occasions. I always say that "hurt people, hurt people." Without even trying, there were times that I hurt my sister, and didn't even understand the reasons behind my actions. Why couldn't I just do what she asked me to do? Most of the time, her requests were simple; I just wouldn't do them. But she loved me despite myself through those times. She saw something in me even when I didn't see it in myself. It would be years before I recognized the divinity in myself—the divinity that she saw in me and in others. I didn't begin to love myself until I was married, with children and far into the path of adulthood.

My journey to discovering the meaning of love was a long and difficult path. I had obviously heard about it, but it was as far as Paris is from America in my heart. Maybe love was difficult for me to understand because, unlike many children, I was not a product of love. Instead, I was the product of rape. My mother had tried to abort me on several occasions through conspicuous methods of her own since abortions were illegal during the sixties. She experienced pain and hemorrhaging for two weeks after thinking that she had succeeded in doing away with an unwanted child. To her surprise Janine A. Ingram was going to be born, despite her attempts to the contrary. What a way to start out life—unwanted, unloved and totally unexpected.

I firmly believe the way I entered this world has shaped how I approach life and its obstacles. I'm *in it to win it*. I'm here, and I'm happy to be here. I recognize and am thankful for the lesson in how I was conceived. And I equally realize that though the beginning was written by several authors who didn't know who or what I would become, the moment I read that single book which sparked those flashes of intuition, purpose, and victory I knew that, despite everything, I was born to be rich.

Now to be honest, rich encompasses many things. Rich in favor, rich in family—like my three beautiful amazing daughters and my wonderful husband who love me unconditionally; my sisters Jessie and Del whose love has been the foundation that has shaped the very essence of who I am today; my nephew Gerard who I love and adore and will always cherish and, my mother Anastasia McAdoo also my godmother Rochelle Knox last but not least, my friends who make the journey of life a little lighter. Rich in purpose such as hosting a conference call that brings nearly one hundred people together every weekday morning to affirm faith, love and purpose.

People tell me all the time that my passion comes through in my prayers, in my speech, in my walk—that it's all around me. This comes not just in spite of, but because of, the many obstacles that I've endured and the many hurdles put out on the track before I was a thought in my mother's womb. Purpose gave life to me and it fills my being with light, love and joy. So I can tell these stories of how life wasn't so kind to me at first, but I can tell you now that with God's grace and mercy that I'm the person writing the vision. I'm the person that God saw fit to give a brush allowing me to paint a beautiful masterpiece of life, stroke by stroke, decision by decision, and every day carving out a brand new wonderful existence.

Although each house I had been shuffled to before living with my sister had its own detriment, they also held a piece in the puzzle of my spiritual journey. In the one house where I was neglected, I learned about prayer. In another house where I was molested and abandoned, I learned about the Bible and the stories of strength and the Wisdom of Solomon. In every home I prayed for wisdom, an attribute that was the furthest thing from any of the adult minds I was connected with. It wasn't until my sister's house that I learned unconditional love and, as I bonded with my other sister, I finally began to understand the meaning of family. It was still much later before it strengthened the foundation of who I AM.

Prayer

Father as I become still and recognize the I Am that I Am, I thank you this morning for the opportunity to come before you one more time. Thank you for the opportunity to learn your word. Thank you for all the things that you have sent my way to teach me how to live spiritually, with virtue and to have an amazing and extraordinary life.

Thank you for that phenomenal opportunity to know today, that I can make a difference in our world. I'm asking for your wisdom, wisdom to become a better friend, a better parent, an extraordinary entrepreneur. Thank you for the blessing you have bestowed upon my life. Father I thank you for the opportunity to bring forth and manifest that Christ Consciousness which resides in me. Thank you for allowing me to share the experiences of how you've been an amazing God in my life. Thank you for teaching me how to love myself. Because when I love myself, the world shows up and loves me as well.

Thank you for teaching me how to remind myself to have loving thoughts, every minute, every second, to remind myself that I am a child of an amazing Father, and that all things that I desire can be mine if I just believe and have faith. Thank you that it only takes the faith of a mustard seed. Thank you for teaching me how to speak life into my world today; for teaching me how to speak boldly and claim my riches, claim my life, claim my health and all my desires. I ask you to open up the windows of Heaven and pour out a blessing. Show up and show out in my life.

Thank you for using me as a vessel to share your words of wisdom. Thank you for allowing me to make a difference in one more person's life. And so it is.

Love Yourself First

I didn't realize that I was not loving Janine A. Ingram. No one could have told me that I didn't love myself, but the proof of that was the fact that I wasn't making decisions that honored me. Yes, I was making a lot of money, but that didn't fulfill the things I really needed, which was love from myself because love comes from a place deep within.

Once I started loving and honoring Janine I was able to face the hard reality of things and situations that needed to be handled. Only then was I able to do things that honored Janine, even in my relationships. I was finally able to face the woman who gave birth to me and say, "Mama, I have to make a change. You must get some help because I love you too much to see you go on this way. You can't stay here in my home. The things you do don't honor me, my home or my children." Once I learned to love Janine, I was able to say no to the things that did not align with truth. No to toxic people in my life, no to foolish financial decisions and no to not taking care of myself. This was all part of the journey of self-discovery. I'm only telling you this to illustrate the point that no matter what we do in life it doesn't mean anything until you learn to love yourself. Then the world opens up and it becomes a more beautiful place. You attract more beautiful things; you attract a better relationship whether it's the same mate or a new one because you're on a whole different level; you learn to discipline your children in love; you learn how to say no in love without allowing anyone to make you feel guilty.

When you start walking in love and living in love and passionately understanding what it means to really truly love yourself from a different perspective, then you understand what it means to have true love. The truth of the matter is that until you have true love, you don't have true peace. Until you have true love you won't have true forgiveness. Because only when you truly love yourself can you forgive yourself and then forgive others. Remember that the Bible says you can't give from an empty vessel. If there is no love inside of you, how can you give it to someone else?

You have to love yourself no matter where you are in life, no matter what or how you feel about yourself. You have to learn to appreciate yourself for the person you are within. No matter the size, the color, the hair—God made you and he made you special. He made you with a purpose.

So many of us walk through this lifetime living in lack of love in your own world. No matter what you do you can't balance love without understanding love. The Universe is only going to come and show you exactly what you're doing. If you're neglecting yourself, you will attract a relationship that neglects you. If you're abusive to yourself, entertaining all kinds of negative talk, you're going to attract exactly what you think about yourself. I'm not good enough. Okay, then you are going to attract something or someone that says you're not good enough. I'm not pretty enough. You're going to attract someone who will tell you that you're not pretty enough or they may point out some other thing that, in their estimation, needs changing.

When you learn to appreciate every part of who you are from head to toe, then that's when the world opens up and learns to appreciate you for who you are no matter what your color or height. When you learn to appreciate you, the world learns to appreciate you. When you learn to love you, the world learns to love you as well. I'm telling you that loving yourself is the most powerful experience you'll ever have. Remember a time when you've been in love; when the window of love opens up and you feel excitement and anticipation. You light up like a Christmas tree and you're so vibrant everyone can see. I remember that feeling, and I would say each time, "God, this is such a fantastic feeling." And it's so wonderful when the world opens up and reminds you what love is.

One day I stepped into the shower and I asked God to heal me and teach me how to love myself. Then I put out there in the Universe that I wanted to be in love with myself the same way it felt when I was in love with someone else. I wanted to wake up saying, "Janine, I love you," and mean it as strongly as if I was speaking those words to another person. I wanted to fix a candlelight dinner for Janine, run that bathwater with bubbles and put the music on just for Janine. I wanted to be in love with myself like that. I can remember praying and meditating every day. It was only through those actions-being still and learning to love Janine that God began to speak to me. I learned what it was, how it is, and what it was all about. Only then did I start on the path of self-discovery that I'm still learning today. I'm probably not one-hundred percent, but I'm getting better and better every day. And so I wanted to share this story with you because I prayed hard to convey the simple meaning of what love is, how powerful it can be and how it can change your life. The loving Father can only do for you what he can do through you, and it's through your own thoughts and feelings of expectation that love is born. As you deliberately express love it comes back to you multiplied.

Think of love as being a radiant light that enfolds and

brightens. Think of love permeating, penetrating and saturating your own being. If you have some dark troublesome areas in your life, think of them as coming alive with the light of Divine love and being Divinely guided by God. There's no reason for feeling guilty about loving yourself. You cannot love others or radiate love to anyone else until you love yourself first. Love begins at home within you. I emphasize the need for self-love and appreciation. Remember, Jesus said, "love the Lord thy God with all thy heart and soul and mind." (Matthews 22:37) This is the greatest first commandment. He was referring to man loving the God nature within himself as well as the Universal God; particularly, to love any part of the body that's crying out for love. Boldly declare to any part of your body that's hurting that God loves you, and therefore you can overcome any situation in your life that's difficult—you can bring about healing.

I say all the time that hurt people, hurt people. When people are hurt and they come into our life, that's just their cry for us to pray for them and to send loving thoughts toward them. Sometimes it's not easy; you might have to step back from the situation and remind yourself that all they might need is a little love. I believe everyone should write out statements in love and affirm those statements in love. Write those love letters whether you send them or not. Just write them out—just like writing your master plan.

Give thanks for every small and large expression of love in your life. By doing so, you release love's multiplying power which can fill every void. Trust love to get you out of your difficulties. Jesus Christ, the master of victorious living, placed a high importance on love. Begin to deliberately generate God's love to yourself, to your family, and to your friends as well as your enemies. As you do, your problems will turn into solutions. You will live a happy, unlimited life.

Prayer

Father, I thank you today for the love you have shown me. Thank you for the journey of self-discovery to teach me how to love myself so I can live more abundantly in love; so that I can walk in love, live in love, discipline my children in love. I can live passionately in love with life, with myself, with those around me. Thank you for the love that you have bestowed upon my life. Thank you for the love for my family, but most importantly thank you for the love I have for myself. I thank you for the sun that shines on my face. Sometimes it gently kisses my face to remind me that I am so loved by you. Today, I ask that you whisper in the ears of my loved ones how much you love them, how magnanimous they are, how powerful and dynamic they are.

Father, today teach me how to live in my purpose, how to love in my purpose, how to walk in my light; so I can share the love and knowledge I've gained with others. Thank you, Father, for the power of love. I declare peace and love in my community; that everyone can see the world turned inside out with that love. And today, I thank you for blessing each and every one of us. Thank you for opening the windows of Heaven and pouring out love in my heart. Thank you for the light of love and that it surrounds and protects me, my family, my loved ones, my employers, and everyone I come in contact with.

And so it is.

Finding True Love

My relationships with men have always been positive. I am grateful for the masculine energy being a pleasant experience whether the relationship was platonic or intimate. One of my first platonic male relationships was with an older man named Pete.

My mother owned three paper stands, and I used to work at the location at 55th and Lake Park on the South Side of Chicago. The opportunity to work at her paper stand allowed me to meet some very fascinating people, and I've always been very appreciative of that fact. Some of the more memorable people I met while working there include: Harold Washington (he used to come to the stand every day before he became the first Black mayor of the city of Chicago); a guy who told me to invest in cell phones back in the 80's because that was going to be the wave of the future (I wish I had been more financially savvy back then and actually listened to the man); and the gentleman who had just started his own magazine called "After Five" who gave me a 10-page spread showcasing a new designer (I was completely fascinated to see myself in a magazine that I actually sold at the paper stand, especially since I used to visualize myself one day being in the various publications). The newsstand is also where I met Pete.

Pete was an older gentleman, around sixty or seventy, who lived in Hyde Park. He stood 6'2"tall had very dark skin and was quite handsome. I could tell that, back in his day, he gave women a run for their money. Pete was also very charming, with extremely soft hands and he was wise to the game of street life. I loved spending time with him and listening to his stories; I learned quite a bit about street life from Pete.

Pete had lived off the Pimp Life. I was completely fascinated by this since I loved to read books like "Iceberg Slim," the "Street Bible," and every book ever written by Donald Goines. These were books on the street hustle, including the pimp game, the drug game and the con game. Pete was someone real, in living color, telling me these stories (that were supposedly true) about street life like those I had loved to read about. I was exhilarated hearing about his endeavors but that is also how I learned to navigate the streets. Pete always warned me to be aware of my surroundings and to always listen intently to what people had to say, but at the same time to be more cognizant of their actions. These were two of the most important life lessons Pete ever taught me—they became my personal code for life. I learned to just watch people. I learned to think about the world as a jungle, full of snakes, lions and tigers, and that only the strong survive; it is a strong person who realizes it is not about emotion, but it's about business.

I learned to be fearless in my dealings because people only respect the bold and confident. I began to always think about what I wanted out of a situation and to make sure that my expectations were known. I learned to always keep my eyes on the prize, on goals I had set for my personal journey. I thank Pete often for the invaluable information he shared with me, and I was able to transfer this knowledge to the business world; his lessons were the key to my success in every workplace. I always moved to the top in record speed.

I learned a lot about survival from Pete but, out of all

the male relationships I have had throughout my life, I am most grateful for my relationship with my husband, Brenton. We have actually known each other since I was in the second grade, but we didn't really start dating until I was 19-years-old. Brenton shaped my life in a whole new way. He is a renaissance man who grew up attending a sanctified church; he is a man of integrity and believes in working hard to attain what is desired.

Brenton has taught me so much: how to cook, how to open a bank account and keep track of spending and how to be a better parent. Brenton is a wonderful father, and the parenting skills he taught me were most effective. He is a man with a great heart, and I've always admired his mind. He has one of the most brilliant minds you ever wanted to encounter and loves to learn, especially when it involves a scientific base. Sometimes I watch him interacting with our beautiful daughters (who are also brilliant, by the way), and I am amazed at the intellectualism that they possess.

Brenton is also a phenomenal cook. He loves to prepare exquisite dishes, but it is nothing for us to go out for a fabulous dinner, take a ride and find beautiful structures and learn about the building's history. Brenton seems to know everything about construction, and he teaches me about the different styles of architecture and who designed them. I came to love Frank Lloyd Wright as a direct result of this type of adventure.

Needless to say, Brenton is an amazing man. I am grateful, because he has always supported anything I desired to do, even when I made mistakes in how I chose to do business. He has never stood in the path of my learning lessons or making a mistake, but he has also shown me how to work myself out of some very costly ideas. For example, I learned a little too late, even though he tried to tell me, that there is no such thing as a "get rich quick scheme"—you end up paying one way or the other.

I have to say that Brenton has been my biggest fan. When I was preparing this book and trying to decide what to say about my wonderful husband, my daughter Ebony happened to call. When I told her what I was doing, she told me excitedly, "I am so looking forward to what you will say about Dad! He has only great things to say about you. Daddy thinks you are one of the most fascinating people he has ever met. He is your biggest fan. Dad said he has never met a more loving person. He said he loves your enthusiasm for life and how you flow effortlessly. Daddy, really, really admires you." So, with that being said, what could a woman do but write?

The Universe is amazing because Ebony's call sparked flashes of inspiration. I had never really heard before how Brenton felt in words. I do know he truly loves and admires me, but it was something else to hear his feeling vocalized by another individual. Brenton was always pushing me to greatness, even when the world was against me and nobody believed or trusted me—Brenton remained true to his game.

Many times when the world knocked me upside the head, he was whispering in my ear to never give up. Even when I was wrong about something, he sent me back in the game pumped up and ready to win. He's always told me that life is like chess; it is an illusion and whoever can bring the best mental game wins. In other words, remember to seek your inner guidance and then move forward.

Brenton is a gentleman, but he's a man's man. I truly enjoy the masculine aura that he possesses. He still opens my door and never lets me carry anything heavy. Brenton always drops me off at the door when we are out some place. I also admire Brenton's strength. For the most part, he is a very calm, dynamic, intellectual person. But, let me tell you, if any hurt, harm or danger were to come around me or our daughters, Brenton becomes a beast that could eat the heart out of any fierce wild animal. Brenton does not play around when it comes to his family.

When I really sit and think about it, I have always been rich! I didn't really see it, however, until I learned to love myself. The love I have in my life is worth more than all the material things I could ever accumulate. I am wealthy; when I look into Brenton's eyes, I know he loves me. When one of my children touches me, speaks to me, or shares something special with me, I can feel their love as well. This is a true reflection of me loving myself.

Prayer

Thank you for the opportunity to be free of negative chatter in my mind. Thank you for the opportunity to release that negative energy and walk in my greatness and walk in your light. Thank you for this journey. Thank you for the support that I have from my loved ones. Thank you for the love I receive from family and friends.

Thank you for teaching me how to walk in love, parent in love, support in love and to be a great friend, and great spouse in your love. Thank you for all of the blessings you have bestowed upon me today. I ask that you teach me and use me as a vessel to help others.

And so it is.

Children are a Gift from God

I have three beautiful daughters, and I like to think that they are the music to my soul. Diamond, my eldest, has a strong personality. She's very giving, loving, supportive and has always been a good girl, but she's also adventurous a lot like me. The one quality that sticks out most to me is that she's such a great big sister; Diamond is a phenomenal role model for her sisters. She always takes time for her sisters, always sharing and being thoughtful to their concerns. When Asia, my youngest, wanted to go away to boarding school, scholarships had been exhausted. The school cost about $35,000 to attend, which was the same amount as the Lexus SUV we had been saving to get Diamond. Well, when it came time to buy her SUV, Diamond said, "Mom, I'll wait for my truck. Go ahead and pay for Asia's school." I had to tell her no, even though I thought it was such an awesome gesture for her to give up something she sorely wanted in order for her sister to have, what she believed, would be a great start in life with a wonderful education full of opportunities. I replied, "No, we will make it happen another way."

Ebony, the middle child, is my "militant, creative, Angela Davis and Nikki Giovanni rolled into one" daughter. There has been only one occasion that I've had any issue with her. It happen to have been when she was actually right. For example, her history teacher was lecturing on various facts, including ones about Christopher Columbus. Well, of course, we all know that history as it is taught in our schools today and the realties of the subject matter do not exactly match up. There are quite a few discrepancies that can be disputed that were once accepted as actual fact, thanks to all of the different texts and other documents that are now readily available.

In his defense, I have to say that the teacher could only teach from the perspective of what he had been taught and the information he had on hand. He certainly didn't realize that there was a student in his midst that had been, on her own volition, taking the time to study and empower herself through the vast recesses of information out there that would back up the fact that Christopher Columbus did not "discover" America among other things. My daughter, who attended a diversely populated school for the Performing Arts, stood in the middle of a lecture and promptly pointed out that, "If you're going to teach history, you need to tell the truth."

The response to her outburst was a call home to me explaining that Ebony was a wonderful student and he's never had a problem with her. But on that day she stood up and went totally off on him, explaining that he needed to learn Black History. And if he's going to teach a history class, he needs to learn it from all perspectives and all cultures—not just his own. He assured me, however, that we could sit down and work it out since she had never been a problem before. Unfortunately, he definitely wanted an apology from her in front of the entire class. Of course, my little militant daughter, who had studied every Black Panther book, every CD, DVD and any other information related to Black History and the history of all people of color. She did not agree with his position, and certainly did not feel the need to apologize. Needless to say, it was challenging explaining to her that the apology was not an admission that what she said was wrong, but was necessary because she had disrespected the teacher in front of all his students.

The next day, I sat in the back of the class as my daughter stood in the front and said, "I would like to apologize for my behavior." And that was all she said. Truthfully, despite what her teacher expected, that was all he was going to get. My daughter is a lot like me, which meant that pressing the issue could have resulted in her just dropping out. When it comes to principles and position, she takes a firm stand. She put the s-t-u-b-b-o and the "r" and the "n" in stubborn. Honestly, her picture should appear right next to that word in the dictionary.

Just so you can get a picture, Ebony wears an afro, and there's hardly ever a day you won't catch her without something that is black, red and green. Fists in the air, anyone? She is an amazing young woman.

Asia, my youngest child, took me by surprise. With my first two girls already on their path, I thought motherhood was a piece of cake—that is until Asia was born. Lord, did this one take me through the ringer! Asia is beyond brilliant, extremely talented and strong-willed (that's not really the best word to describe her nature). God had to come down from Heaven and tell Asia not to do something. She challenged me to learn how to become a better mother, and I'm grateful for that.

Asia is the type of person that once she sets her mind on accomplishing something she won't stop until she's made it happen. One memorable example of this is when she decided she wanted to attend boarding school instead of the local area schools or even the top magnet schools and performing arts schools her sisters had attended. I wasn't thrilled at the idea; in fact, I had serious issues with it. I thought boarding schools were for bad kids or the reprieve of parents who didn't know how to be a parent or have time for their children. I tried to explain this to her and told her I loved her too much and didn't want her to go away at fourteen years of age. I thought she would understand my point of view. Boy, was I wrong!

Asia was in a program for gifted children, and she managed to get herself into a high school fair for private schools and boarding schools. When I picked her up later in the day, I could tell immediately she was excited about something. As soon as she sat in the car, she proceeded to tell me the reason she was so excited. "Mom, I know you said you didn't want me to go away to school, but I want you to open your mind and hear me out." Then she hit me with, "Ma, it resonated with my spirit." Humph! I can only guess that she made note of my solemn expression as she added, "Ma, for real. This is the school I want to go to." Of course, she didn't apply to any other high school. She was accepted, but unfortunately there wasn't any scholarship money available. Despite my refusal to allow her older sister to forego her car to put the money on Asia's education, things worked out for her to attend, but it didn't come easy. That's another story in and of itself.

Having three amazing daughters has been an inspiration in my life. They uplift me, they give me so much joy and pleasure I never knew existed. I always say that Diamond taught me love, Ebony taught me patience, and Asia gave me wisdom. The most fascinating aspect of it all is that even with how very unique they are, I see myself in each and every one of them. The bottom line is that at one point in time they gave me a reason to continue the journey every day. There were days when it was hard to get up, take one to one school, then the other two to another, then to gymnastics, saxophone lessons, piano lessons, violin lessons, soccer practice, basketball practice, and countless other venues. Every waking moment was filled with doing something for or with my daughters. I even found jobs that allowed the flexibility to maintain that rigorous schedule. I kept plenty of books in the car so when I dropped one off, I sat there and read until the next one called, and so on. As J. L. Woodson, one of my favorite young authors said, one has to learn to "circle until you land." And Lord, I was circling Chicago like a 747 jet!

Children especially thrive on sincere appreciation, praise and encouragement. It is important that we remember that we must discipline our children in love. That doesn't mean that you don't work to correct negative behavior or discipline them, but you should be firm, yet loving, in your discipline. The root of the word discipline means to perfect. Your method of correction and discipline should lead to perfection rather than to rebellion, resistance, or other negative behavior. Pray for Divine guidance concerning each one of your children. This is true education.

One thing we always want to do as parents is seek God's wisdom for our children's life. I remember when I watched different television shows or movies where the children in them were practically uncontrollable, and I would think, "They just need a whipping. That's all." But if the goal is to discipline our children in love, then that's not true. And life brought that lesson home. Some kids you can't whip into the right direction. Some kids, no matter what you do, just don't respond to corporal punishment or any other type of punishment. I learned that from my youngest daughter. One day I just said, "God, what is going on?" One of her teachers said to me, "I wanted all your children in my class because you have amazing children."

Then this strange expression came over her face as though she was weighing how to phrase her next statement. "But I wanted to ask you, is this one yours?" I had to laugh at her question as I answered, "Yeah, she's mine, too. I just don't know where she came from." But the amazing thing about it is Asia taught me patience. She taught me how to be still and seek God's wisdom.

One day she made me so angry that I couldn't even see straight. That's when I really understood the saying "still waters run deep" because I was so upset I couldn't even talk. I just sat there and looked at her. I couldn't believe my daughter was so hard-headed. Yes, I know you're thinking, "but isn't she just like you?" As a matter of fact, she is. However, I wasn't seeing it quite that way at the time.

At that moment when I was so furious with her, I became very still and start praying. Then I had a long conversation with her but God gave me the words to say. My daughter cried so hard anyone looking in would have thought that I had done some physical damage, but I hadn't touched her. It was just that the words convicted her heart. From that day forward our relationship changed; there's a whole different pattern now. I came to understand that I had to reach her mind. I had to seek God's wisdom to do it or she would have been too out of control and, I'm sorry to say, I would've been too embarrassed to say she was mine.

We, as parents, need to teach our children that God never intended them to fail or to live in lack or to be lacking. It's really very important that we let every child know that there's greatness inside of them, that every gift that has come to them is received as a gift from God. Remind them that they are a gift from God every single day.

One night my friend Lissa, was moved when she heard me having a conversation with my daughter where I said, "Please yourself, not me." Our relationship had changed and grown as she entered into adulthood, yet she was still trying to please me. I had to remind her that she was an adult now, and she had to learn to please herself. If that meant I wasn't pleased, then I would need to learn to get over it. "You have to live your life for you."

Now, at the time of this writing, I'm in transition. Diamond graduated from the University of Michigan and landed a position with the city while working on her masters from a prestigious university. Ebony is currently at a top Historically Black College (still as culturally conscience as ever!) and working on a degree in performing arts and journalism. Asia is currently a senior at the boarding school she convinced me was in her best interest (Miss "It resonated with my spirit!"). She is president of her student body, is loved by all faculty and staff and is also an honorary chair of the disciplinary committee which helps make major decisions in regards to the student body. All three of my daughters have traveled abroad—Paris, Italy, South Africa and Australia, and soon to China and other countries.

Each one of them is now on their own journey and path. There is no longer a need for me to shuffle between classes and practice; no need to put someone else's time before my own. Instead, I'm learning to put me on my own "to do" list and that is a major task within itself—especially when you've been a giver all your life. You give as a wife, you give as mother, you give as an employee, you give as a family member, and you give as a friend. There's been so much giving that there hasn't been much time or opportunity for receiving. Along my journey,

I've learned that this is an issue I share with a great majority of women. We are givers by nature because we've been taught to be that way by our mothers, grandmothers, teachers and ministers. There are times when we'll see women going to spas and getting massages, facials, pedicures and manicures—that's because they put themselves on their "to do" list, as we all should.

Being an empty nester has forced me to take a look at my life as it relates to me and my career as well. Learning to live without the rigorous schedule, making sure everything was taken care of for everyone else, that now the focus is on me. Since the spotlight is on me, it's so difficult for me to focus on me—to put me on the "to do" list. I have to always rewind life a little bit and say, "Hey, you forgot something YOU!" They say it takes twenty-one days to break a habit, but I'm not quite sure that it's working in this regard. I keep asking myself when am I going to put Janine A. Ingram on the "to do" list without having to remind myself to do it?

I am taking steps in the right direction, venturing to dance classes—modern dance, pole dancing (hey, I AM married, you know!) and I'm going back to school to become certified as a life coach. I'm taking it one day at a time, learning to enjoy me and trying to live in the moment, because I've come to realize transitioning is a bumpy ride. What's even more challenging is to suddenly actually live IN what you say, such as: "Depend on the Universe, because the Universe is friendly to our desires" or "Walk by faith…"—it's frightening at first. But I'm excited and have a peaceful feeling about the next phase of my life. I have no doubt in the world that MY BEST IS YET TO COME!

This is where I will truly become ME. I'm excited to go forward into the next phase of my life with the feeling of peace.

I will truly blossom in these next chapters of my LIFE!

Prove me now herewith said Jehovah of hosts, if I would not open you the windows of Heaven and pour you out a blessing that there shall not be room enough to receive it.

(Malachi 3:10)

And all things are possible to him that believeth.

(Mark 9:23)

With God all things are possible.   (Matthew 19:26)

Prayer

Thank you for the youth who are beginning to understand the spiritual laws of prosperity. Thank you for the opportunity for them to create a vision board, to create their goals and envision their dreams at a very young age so they can live an amazing life; so they can understand that by the words they speak, the thoughts they keep, is how they create their world.

Thank you for the opportunity to raise their consciousness and understand that we can have all things. Thank you that we know that we can become still and know that you are God. Thank you for giving us and bestowing your wisdom upon us. And for that we say thank you.

Amen.

Create a Vision Board and Design a Master Plan

I first learned about vision boards when I was seventeen and attended Christ Universal Temple. They called it "Treasure Mapping" and so does Catherine Ponder. My first vision board consisted of an affirmation of graduating from high school. The rest were material things: cars, clothes, shoes (I'm a shoe-a-holic!), jewelry and accessories—the works for any growing young woman. My second vision board was completed when I was in my twenties. It was an affirmation of getting my real estate license (even then I thought I was going to be rich!).

Rich is relative to what you think rich is at the time. It's easy to get caught up in the material trappings, so once again, it was about what I drove. I had a 1988 1/2 BMW M3 (they made it later in the year, so it couldn't be called an '88, and it wasn't quite an '89—so the car was a 1988 and a half), 5 speeds with the works. It didn't hurt that the car was also fire engine Red. I had an apartment in Hyde Park on the board as well. I thought I was doing the dag on thang (as my children would say).

I moved to Hyde Park with my new car, and I got a real estate license—all in a matter of two months. I thought I was all set. I didn't know, unfortunately, that it was going to take - six whole months to close that first real estate deal. In other words, I didn't have a dime during that time frame. Now I had a car and a car note as well as an apartment with a rent payment, all at twenty-two years old without even two nickels to rub together. I think this is a good point to say that we should teach our children financial responsibility. I didn't even know how to write a check, let alone open a checking account or balance a checkbook. And to make matters more interesting, here came my first experience with credit. I had a Marshall Field's credit card and a Visa—dangerous tools in the hands of a young woman with no financial wisdom.

I was laying in the bed every night doing my prayers and affirmations. I'm grateful to the Universe because I had a lot of people who loved me and supported my not quite bad, but not quite wise, habits.

When that first commission check came through it was in the amount of $25,000, and I was in the position to pay everybody back. I was in college at the time and an earth angel (of course, it was Brenton, the love of my life) taught me how to open a bank account, balance my checkbook and even to put money in a Certificate of Deposit. He even taught me how to cook! The major lesson I learned is that it takes a while for deals to close and for the money to land in my hand, so I should act accordingly. I did better the second time around, and even better the third time around, but it was still a learning process.

My next vision board came along when I decided to step up my game. I wanted a Lexus LS 400 with leather seats, CD player, sunroof—all the bells and whistles, and I was all excited to have it. The vision board class I attended was interesting and opened a world of possibilities for me. The teacher told us a story of a woman who put a black and white picture of a travel destination on her vision board. She got the trip, but it rained the entire time!!! We were encouraged to make sure to put the specific picture in living color.

You didn't have to tell me twice. I took a big poster-size picture of that Lexus from the dealer and put it on my wall. And guess what? About three months later I was driving down the street in my Audi, and the Lexus in question was on display at a dealership, elevated on a rotating display high above all the other cars. Right car, right color, right make, fully-loaded and everything! I was in Heaven. I told everyone, including a certain friend, that I had seen the car of my dreams. Two weeks later he won some money and went to pick the car up and gave it to me as a gift. Now how cool was that? My second Lexus came to me the same way. By that time the Lexus of my dreams (which I aptly named Big Poppa) had about 300,000 miles on it and was starting to go through some mid-mile life changes. So I put a pearl white, 2-door SC-400 Lexus with tan leather seats and sunroof on my vision board.

My mechanic came over one day to see what was going on with Big Poppa, and he drove up in the exact Lexus I had on my board. I looked at the car because it was calling my name Janine, Janine, Ja.....nine! While he was attending to my car, I was across the way checking out his car. He ended up having to drop me off at my destination in his car. I said to him, "I feel like this is my car." He said, "No, this car isn't for sale." I nodded and said, "but I know this is my car. It spoke to me and everything." Folks might think I'm a little off, but they see the results and don't say too much when I talk this way.

The mechanic tried to get me to buy a Mercedes he had for sale, but I wasn't having it. Days later Big Poppa was still "sick," and the mechanic was still trying to get me to buy something else. Two weeks, three days and four hours passed and I finally got a call, "Janine, the car's for sale. I'm going to drop it off to you." So, I'm driving my new car—with more toys than I had requested on the board. Yes, indeed! Now the only challenge I faced was where to get the funds to pay for it. I fasted and prayed...and fasted and prayed some more. I was almost at the point where I was going to have to give the car back to my mechanic, and I was telling a friend about how everything had come to pass. That friend simply asked, "How much do you need?" I put the mechanic on the phone, and he gave my friend the amount. My friend told me to come and pick up a check the next day. Now, those are the types of friends who truly had my back. I would also learn through my journey, that not all friends are like this.

A vision board should have an image of things you want to create in your world. This is a world that we are creating on our vision board, and it should be extraordinary. You want to create abundance, so remember when you're putting things on your vision board, make sure those things are positive and things that you want to create in your life; that it doesn't have anything to do with pain or hurt. We don't want to attract things that hurt, that repel, and that are negative.

If you do not constantly have confidence that your desires can come true, place a picture of that desired result where you can view it daily. Your subconscious mind will make it so that your visions will come to pass.

I find it interesting that people call me with questions regarding the vision boards. "What date should I put down that I want my debts to be paid?" Only you can answer that. Set that date and trust in God to send the money or resources. It's about unexpected prosperity, and God can only do for you what he can do through you. He is only as big as your faith. When we limit God, we limit our lives.

Let go of having to figure out how things will get done.

People don't really understand what "let go and let God" means. They really don't understand what it means to lean not to your own understanding. They'll say, "Okay, I'm going to put my bills in here, but I think it'll take me about two years to pay that." Then if that's what you believe, because God is faith in action, and if your faith is that it will take two years to pay this off, then that's what you put on your vision board and that's exactly what will happen.

There's a woman in my Intender's Circle who put together a game plan to have all debts paid in full by spring 2010 at the time of this writing. Every day she sees a demonstration of manifestation of something that helps facilitate that process. She's landed new clients which equates to more income. Some debts were reduced on their own; others, upon checking into them, were found to be unsubstantiated. She put some emotion behind that request that all debts are paid in full at little or not cost to her and by her timeline. She even shared her timeline with her young son so he could do the same. Now he's been pulling in more clients and handling bills, knocking them off his list. They're not trying to limit and say, "well, my paycheck will have it all done by xyz," they leave the details to the Creator.

Remember your vision boards are to be clear and precise, and exactly what we want to bring forth in life just by simply asking our Father for guidance. Our Father is such a loving father and no matter where you are in the game, don't ever think that you're not worthy to stop and ask God for anything. Wherever you are, you're worthy enough to be on this earth; you were worthy the moment God created you. So never think you're not spiritual enough, or good enough to just stop and ask God for the answer. God will answer faster than you think,

I promise you that much.

Really think about when you're putting together your master plan, creating your vision boards, envisioning your wonderful life, to not think about your own understanding. Don't limit your thoughts. It's really important that we believe and have faith in what we're doing. People text me asking, "Why are we saying these affirmations over and over? What's the purpose?" There's so much power in the spoken word, and I don't think people understand the ramifications of what the power of the spoken word is all about. There's more power in the spoken word than any other thing that we can do in our life. Affirming and decreeing and claiming boldly that we want peace, harmony, love, prosperity, joy, abundance means that everything in the Universe sets in motion to bring that about.

When you are stating affirmations, focus on the emotional part of everything. It's important that you think about the emotions behind your affirmation. For example, if you decide to use the affirmation "I can do all things through Christ who strengthens me," how you say it can really make a difference in how it is perceived by the Universe. Whether you simply say it or whether you exclaim it, like "I CAN DO ALL THINGS THROUGH CHRIST WHO STRENGTHENS ME!" it's important that the emotions within you come forth through your affirmation. It is also important that we use our emotions as a measure to understand if we're actually feeling what we're saying with desire, or just saying them to be saying them. That's the key ingredient to attracting and claiming your prosperity because the emotional part of it is vital. The feelings behind the words, is what brings forth the manifestation, the energy. If you're not feeling what you're affirming, then they just become words.

Some have the discipline when they first start out, there's

this emotion-packed drive. Then when things start flowing, they'll start taking things for granted, lose momentum, and then lose that emotion behind those desires. Don't have your emotions all scattered. You have to remember to stay focused—mentally, emotionally and spiritually—and concentrate on the area that you want to create in your life. Focus in on your affirmations and on your plan. At this point, you should have a master plan for your life. Even if you haven't created a vision board, you definitely should have written down the desires of the amazing life you want to have for yourself. It's imperative to have a written plan because it's a map; it's a guide to the direction that you want to have for your life.

You wouldn't travel to Florida and decide to just get in a car without knowing which direction you're heading, yet that is exactly what you're doing when you don't have a master plan for your life. If there's a desire for your life and you want to attain certain goals, write them down then create a map of the direction you want to take in order for you to get there. Once you have created the map and written down your detailed goals, then make it more concise and straight to the point of what you desire for life. It's amazing how the Universe brings the right people at the right time to give you exactly what you need to create that amazing life. God is so amazing that way.

There are three powerful tools: speaking it into existence, writing it down and visualizing it. Simply put: pictures, spoken words and written words. These are the tools to achieving success. These three things are the most powerful ways to manifest anything in this world. Once you speak it into the Universe, once you have written it down and you see it in your mind, people just show up. You might be sitting next to a person and it might be the very person who can help you to get what you need. For example, one week I had a talk with my niece and found out that she wanted to go to Columbia College. My friend, Nikki, owns a shoe store. I walked into her store not too long after that conversation with my niece, and Nikki had so many customers that she couldn't help them all. So I pitched in and started helping out. One of the customers I was working with struck up a conversation as we handled the transaction. Guess where she worked? Columbia College! Needless to say, she became a very important piece of the puzzle because she was able to help facilitate my niece in filling out the necessary paperwork and following the procedures to get into Columbia.

On another day she expressed a desire to write a book. As we left a vision board class, we stopped at Nikki's store and her cousin walked in talking about the book he had written and that he was available to help get her book together. He gave her some very definitive steps to start her in the right direction. It's completely amazing that once you put a goal into the Universe, the Universe just touches other people to help you, or you might "coincidentally" end up sitting next to the right person. Keep in mind that there really is no such thing as a coincidence; everything happens, the way it happens, for a reason.

Don't be afraid to think big. We have a Father that is magnanimous. He's larger than life, bigger than we can ever imagine. His reach is unlimited! Don't be afraid to ask God for exactly what it is you desire. Sometimes his thoughts, goals and dreams for you are way bigger than what you want for yourself. Seeking his wisdom is important. There's nothing on this earth outside of yourself that can give you the answer and solution to the things you need than being still and seeking the wisdom of God. Sometimes when I go in my own little world where I'm fasting, praying and seeking his wisdom, he just gives me so much clarity. He speaks to me. He tells me exactly what to do to achieve what I need.

Every now and then you have to stop and just be still. Sometimes you have to go all into yourself, be quiet and seek God's wisdom. Cut the television off, cut the phone off, lock the door. If the only place you can have a moment's peace is the bathroom, then run some bathwater, relax and think so you can be receptive to God's wisdom. Allow Him to work through you. When you allow God to work through you, your life will change for the better. My daughter always tells this joke, if you want God to have a good laugh, tell Him your plan for your life. And that's true, because, God's plan for our lives is much bigger than we can begin to imagine.

Prayer

Thank you for teaching me how to eat from the rich, radiant buffet of life. Thank you for the amazing opportunity to share my life with those who share my vision. Thank you for preparing the table of success and that my cup runneth over. Thank you for making this day an amazing day. Thank you for reminding me that I'm your child and that you love me unconditionally. Thank you for the opportunity to share this wisdom and gifts with my children, with my mate, with my family and friends. Thank you that we all have the opportunity to live amazing lives.

And so it is.

Learn from Your Mistakes: The FBI Story

Prosperity comes in its own time. Since I was armed with all these great tools, I tried to force prosperity to come to me. I once owned a mortgage company and an insurance company. I was one of the coldest financial wizards anyone could ever meet when trying to close a deal. It didn't matter if a credit report contained repossession, bankruptcy or foreclosure—I was able to get practically anyone financed. Some called me The Woman with The Midas Touch, meaning that everything I put my hands on turned to gold. I believe a lot of it had to do with the fact that I was great at developing relationships which led to connections in the banking industry, the insurance industry, and the real estate industry. In my mind, I thought I had it going on! I was making six figures, driving a Benz, went shopping any time I wanted and owned ten properties—the majority of them in the South Deering area. I was labeled the Queen of Jeffery Manor. One thing I soon learned about life, however, is that the tastes for material trappings sometimes obscures the need for healing. Life has a funny way of showing up and slapping you upside the head just when you think you have it all figured out. This time my lesson came in the form of the FBI knocking on my door.

My business partner had made some bad real estate moves which caused the FBI to take a closer look at our professional dealings and our personal finances. They shut down everything, including business and personal bank accounts, so they could make heads or tails of the situation. Whether we had been naughty or nice, we were out of business until they could figure out exactly what he—and by association, I—had been up to. It was at this point in my life that I learned the very hard lesson that my grandmother tried to instill in me as a child "when you lay down with dogs, you come up with fleas." In this case it was a major infestation, and I was itching all over.

The FBI investigation couldn't have come at a worse time. My partner had just taken out a loan from a private investor to buy a group of foreclosures properties, and we owed him $100,000. We were at a complete loss because the FBI had halted all incoming cash flow. With my professional life in complete mayhem, everything in my personal life also started to unravel. I began to recognize problems in my relationship with my husband, my mother and even with myself. The only relationships I was able to maintain were the ones with my children. No matter what happened in life, my children and I always kept a stable relationship. In an attempt to salvage something from my old life, I tried finding different ways to stay afloat. Things still continued falling apart. My Midas Touch had become a myth as everything I touched no longer turned to gold but to dust, slipping through my fingers like grains of sand. My relationship with the bank shattered, my business relationships suffered, trust was broken and people turned their backs on me.

It was during this time of professional and personal strife that I remembered what an old man had once told me "there's nothing like the loudness of the silence of your friends when you need them most." And let me tell you, it was quiet from every friendship corner of my world. No matter how hard I defended my integrity to my so-called friends, it only seemed to fall on deaf ears. It wasn't until after everything was said and done that people came around, claiming they had my back. Really? I couldn't tell. These people said they knew I would be victorious, but it would have been nice to hear that when it mattered and not when the battle was over.

As life would have it, this would serve as a cleansing process of allowing me to let go of everything toxic—including people, issues and things. I was being torn down so I could be rebuilt. This catastrophic event served as a major learning experience for me. For one, I most definitely did not have the Midas Touch. But what I did have was God existing inside of me. Growing up in a sanctified church and attending Catholic school taught me to believe in a God, sitting high and looking low. I stayed prayerful and I meditated for redirection and understanding giving way to my REBIRTH. Today I understand that it was God using me to create all of the things I had accomplished.

It took losing everything that once mattered to me to realize what was really important in life; to learn that God was inside me, and everywhere, at once. Just when I thought things couldn't get any worse, my daughter fell extremely ill and the doctors didn't think she was going to live. In fact, at one point during her nine week stay they told me to prepare myself to say goodbye. I was devastated. The most frustrating aspect of the entire situation was that her pain and sickness was preventable. You see, Diamond became ill when her appendix burst and for four weeks toxins invaded her body.

We had been back and forth to four different emergency rooms each time she experienced pain, and each time we were told she had the stomach flu. But a mother's intuition can trump even a doctor's diagnoses, and I refused to accept it was just the flu. One afternoon I drove to Diamond's school early and ate my lunch in my car as I waited for her. She had insisted on going to school despite her pain. No stomach flu was going to keep her from maintaining her top grade point average!

It was a blessing in disguise because as soon as I pulled up, one of her friends called and told me that she had passed out in the restroom. I ran into the school and made it to the bathroom where my little girl laid on the cold industrial tile floor. My heart leaped into my throat as I picked her up and ran down the stairs to the car. I rushed her to one of the three hospitals that had seen her before. They, like the other two, had sent her away saying that her pain was merely the result of the stomach flu.

When I arrived, they saw her and tried to tell me once again that it was just the stomach flu. I was not going to let them get rid of us that easily this time around. I stood my ground and told them, "No! I'm not leaving this hospital until something makes sense. This is NOT the stomach flu." My child was not the type to make up an illness—she was in serious pain and I wasn't going to sit back and watch her suffer any longer. At that moment nothing else mattered, not the FBI, not the loss of my businesses and certainly not the loss of my properties. Nothing mattered but my lovely daughter. Her illness put things completely in perspective. She, along with my other two daughters, is the most important thing in my life and no amount of money can ever change that.

By midnight the doctors had come back with three different diagnoses, but none of them felt right to me. By my insistent requests, they re-evaluated her yet again, and this time they performed an MRI. Finally the mystery started to unfold. Diamond's appendix had burst and the poisons had taken over her little body. Some of the toxins were clustered an inch away from her heart so surgery was out of the question. If they opened her up, the toxins could spread and she would die instantly. Our best option was to insert a tube inside of her to try to drain the poison. That worked, but only for a short time. In the middle of the night the poisons fought back and took over again, forcing the doctors to perform emergency surgery. However, they didn't hold out any hope that she would survive.

Those doctors didn't know my Diamond, my precious gem. My daughter was a fighter and survived the first surgery allowing the doctors an opportunity to go in and drain some of the poisons as well as clean up a few things. Yet it still wasn't enough to heal her completely. In order for my daughter to be a happy and healthy little girl again, they would need to do another surgery that required them to remove pieces of the appendix and drain the rest of the toxins. The catch was there was still so much poison in her body that there was only a fifty-fifty chance she would survive. We had faith in God and the doctors so we agreed to the surgery. She came out of it, thank God, but she was hooked up to machines pumping her with pain medication for days. Each day she was in a somber mood and didn't seem to be getting any better.

I had been fighting the process on all fronts. I tried to deny that my child was deathly ill, while desperately attempting to hold on to all of my properties. Scrambling to figure out how to pay the bills, and on top of all that, I had to deal with the realization that I needed to tell my mother that she would have to go into rehab. To make matters even worse I didn't have any medical insurance. The bills from my daughter's health scare were piling up faster than income was flowing in to pay for them. The harder I tried to hold onto Diamond and the harder I worked to keep everything else together, the further everything seemed to slip away. The doctors kept coming into her room saying that it was a day-by-day walk of faith, hoping she would make it through each night. And I was praying to God every night to please allow me to keep my daughter. God, please.

After many stressful nights at the hospital, I went home to take a shower and called my friend Renae. She listened as I cried and I released all the emotions I'd tried to deny for so long. I prayed to God every night, begging Him to let me keep my daughter. Renae told me about a gospel song titled, "Stand" with the lyrics "When you've done all you can do—stand." As she spoke the words they went from her mouth to my ear and spoke to my soul. I hung up the phone, and I looked at everything—the home where I lived, the pictures of each one of my properties and I evaluated my mother's situation and all the efforts that it had taken to keep her out of trouble. I assessed the heartbreak for my daughter—I was so devastated in the fact that I could lose her. I just couldn't imagine life without my precious Diamond.

I went down on my knees, and I told God, "I'm willing to let go of whatever you want me to let go of—even if that means the most precious gift you gave me—my daughter. If this is God's will, let it be done." I prayed and I asked God to give me the strength, the courage and the will to live without her. And I just couldn't see it at the time; the mere thought was too painful. I asked God to help me make it through.

That night was the first night I spent away from the hospital since she had been admitted. The next morning I got up, took my shower, washed my hair and all the while I praised God for his will to be done. When I arrived back at the hospital,

I immediately noticed a change. There had been days when I would look into her face and her spirit was dim, it was as if someone had extinguished her light. But on this particular day, her light was shining through and I knew she was going to make it. It was the first day Diamond was able to get up out of the bed and walk. The doctors, who hadn't held out any hope, proclaimed it a miracle. Yet even with that spark of recovery, they thought she would be in the hospital for two to three more months. By the grace of God she was only in for nine weeks.

I had allowed the material trappings to make me believe I had power to make things happen, instead of realizing that it was God in me that made everything happen. I had lost sight of what was really important.

While exploring Buddhism concepts and teachings, I heard the statement, "It is when you know nothing that you know everything." It took me many years before I fully understood the true meaning of that statement. We limit God by not opening our minds or expanding ourselves because, as we so aptly put it, we already know everything. The glass is already full so nothing else can be poured into it. But after that night, on my knees, those words resonated in my spirit —it's not until you let go of everything—that you gain everything.

In the surrendering process, I learned not only what it really meant to seek the Kingdom, but also what it really meant to love myself. I realized it had nothing to do with getting my nails and hair done every week, the kind of car I drove, where I lived, the amount of money in my bank accounts. Rather it had everything to do with the spirit. While on my journey to self-discovery I grew to understand that our Father, our Mother, the Creator, the Universe, is friendly to our desires and that means living a happy, fulfilling and abundant life. But first we must allow our purpose to flow through us and then we must recognize the true source of power.

You see in some strange way, I thought that I, Janine A. Ingram, the real estate queen—the Midas Touch Woman—was in control. I didn't think God showed up on time; he seemed like he was always a little late so I said, "That's all right, God, I got this. See, I know how to make this happen." I quickly found out I was very wrong. In his own way He made his presence known. Saying "No, Janine. I'm the one who makes things happen. You see, purpose gave life to you. You didn't give life to purpose."

I heard His words loud and clear in all that happened in my life that year. Those growing pains of having that lesson slammed home is one of the reasons that I am ever so grateful to allow the grace of God to work through me and be used as His servant today. What's most amazing is that no matter what's happening on the outside, nothing takes away the peace that lives inside of me. It was a hard lesson to learn, but I'm glad to have learned it. Once I learned to love myself and to let God take over, I was able to find what I had been missing—peace, love and joy.

Now that this challenge with my eldest child was over, there were still all the other things in my life to deal with. But I knew if God could handle the big things—like allowing my daughter to live despite how bleak things looked during her illness—then the FBI and that persistent private investor was a piece of cake.

The FBI had some boundaries to consider. The private investor, more aptly known as a loan shark, that my business partner had engaged, had no boundaries. At this point, the partner in question who had started it all and had kept me in the dark about more than a few things was now sitting in a place where no one likes to be—Club Fed. Consequently, he also left me holding the purse—an empty designer one at that. Of course, the private investor didn't care who had originated that loan; he wanted his money, and he wanted it right then and there.

He would sit outside my house, trying to frighten me and my family, waiting for me to come home. One night, I just invited him on in and said, "Hey, let's talk about this." The fact of the matter is that he and his entourage walked in my home with guns as big as all get out strapped to their sides. Despite knowing this, I managed to have the courage to say, "You're sitting out there intimidating me and threatening me is not going to help me get your money any faster. What we need to do is come up with some realistic time frames that I can get you your money back, even though I wasn't the one who borrowed the money from you." He didn't say anything at this point, just shared a glance with his buddies. Not sure what to make of their expressions, I pressed on and added, "Killing me is not going to get your money back." He looked a little sheepish at hearing that statement.

My husband was home at the time and stood silently by, watching me the entire time as I talked to this man, trying to explain what was what. Unfortunately for me, my wonderful husband had plenty to say when they left my house! He knew I was a risk-taker and had supported me in a great many things—but this peril took him off guard. My dealings with my now ex-partner had jeopardized our family and our safety. I never intended for this to happen, but now that it had landed on my plate, it wasn't going away easily. I would need to do everything I could to rectify this situation . . . and quickly. The meeting served to at least put a plan of action in place and take the first steps in the right direction.

Now it was time to deal with the mysterious FBI. You might think everything's all good with them, and then they call you six months later and pull the rug out from under you. But it was two years before all the pieces fell together for the FBI and they hauled me into court. What they found within those two years of investigation was a discrepancy on the mortgage application of the very first foreclosure I had purchased and that was enough for them to come after me. I had hired an attorney to handle the paperwork and hearings until a date was set when I had to appear in court for a final determination before the judge. My attorney wasn't exactly optimistic and told me to prepare myself for a judgment of either six months in Club Fed or house arrest.

The night before the court date, a few of my girlfriends came over and offered to take me out in an attempt to cheer me up. We headed to 3Gs—a stepper's club in the south suburbs—and as much as I love to dance, I was kind of teary-eyed, concerned for my fate. Anyone who really knows me, though, knows that I really do love to dance. So, despite my fears for the future, I walked on the dance floor. As I was out there stepping, that smooth Chicago dance style the most amazing thing happened—a song came on, one that I have danced to on many occasions, but I had never before that time, really listened to the words. Faith Evans' soulful voice imparting the lyrics "God's got your back" resonated within my soul. It seemed as if everything around me stood still and those words were the only things in my world. Chills went down my spine and I felt a warm presence, like a vibration holding me, which lifted my spirit. Deep down I knew God was telling me, point blank, "I've got your back."

The next day as I prepared to appear in court, those words still loudly resonated in my ear, as if God himself was trying to make sure I got the message. When I arrived in the courtroom, the whole place was filled with my friends and family. I started saying the Our Father prayer repeatedly in my mind, and then I closed my eyes and went into a deep meditation.

When I opened my eyes, I heard my attorney's voice speaking passionately about my childhood; what I had gone through and how I had became this wonderful person, a wonderful mother with three brilliant children. As I heard him speak about the different chapters of my life, I peered around the room and my heart stood still when I saw that everybody—from the court reporter to the judge—was crying. For the first time, I heard someone else describing what I had gone through and where I had come from, and I felt humble as I realized everything I had overcome. I reflected on the fact that there are so many people who have gone through more than I and some that may have experienced a lot less; but it is those experiences, those challenges, that fashion us, shape us and mold us into the amazing individuals we are destined to be.

When my attorney finished talking about my life, somehow I knew that everything was going to be all right, just like the words in the song I'd heard the night before at the club. As the judge gathered his wits and looked out at everyone present, preparing to address the court, the prosecuting attorney suddenly broke the mood by asking to see my tax returns. The judge allowed everyone to take a recess instead.

When the prosecutor realized the charges he had filed against me were not going to stick, in a fit of rage and desperation he asked to review my taxes for fraud. After three hours of investigating my taxes for the past ten years, they found that everything was in order. I was fined because of the discrepancy on the paperwork of that foreclosure, but I was now a free woman! I could go home with my family. God truly did have my back!

Prayer

As I become still and recognize your presence in my life, I want to thank you for giving me the strength, the courage and the wisdom to do your will. I thank you for giving me the courage to allow my greatness to shine, to set the champion within me free. Build my self-confidence, Father, so I can learn how to walk in your love and walk in your light.

I ask you today to give me the strength, the courage and the wisdom to do your will; to allow the presence of Christ to manifest in my life today. Father I ask you to let the words that come from my mouth be of you and be about you. Today, I want to be a vessel for you, Father, to just walk in your light. I ask that you give me a clean heart and renew the right spirit within me. As I walk in your presence and as I walk in your light, and recognize that your presence, the I Am that I Am, exists in each in every one of us today. Thank you for your angels that walk beside me. Thank you for the love deep inside of me.

And so it is.

Finding Power Through Self-Confidence

If prosperity could be described in one expression, what would it be? Self-confidence. Success states that there's tremendous power in self-confidence, which doubles your power and multiplies your ability, just in the idea of believing in yourself. Success is even more remarkable when we realize that all we have to do is believe in ourselves, which basically boils down to having faith in your own innate abilities and talents. The secret to self-confidence is that you already have it. It's a part of your spiritual nature which you were endowed with when you were created in the image and likeness of God. Remember that you were made a little lower than an, angel who was made with glory and honor and that the Master has written "Ye are Gods." (John 10:34)

The truth that we are born with confidence can be viewed by the actions and reactions of most children. Before they become filled with the fears, phobias and inhibitions put upon them by their elders, children have a delightful habit of confidently saying and doing whatever they feel. A brilliant child who has low self-confidence does not possess half the potential as an average child with a good degree of self-confidence.

There are many times when we take things out of God's hands thinking that we can control them, thinking that we can do a better job than what He can do. But self-confidence gives us the understanding that if we just release and let go and have faith, God will work it out.

The very air that you're breathing and the world in which you live in is filled with Divine Intelligence. If you seek that inner-being, you will know all that you wish to know about everything and that same Divine Intelligence will perform wonders for you. You have to have self-confidence to succeed. You have to believe in yourself and in your ability to succeed; self-confidence breeds success. You have to have an inner ear to listen for God and his wisdom. When you have faith, you will radiate poise and assurance that will surround you and people will naturally believe in your dreams, and follow your ideas and invest in them. Having self-confidence, loving yourself, becoming great and allowing yourself to move past your fears and any obstacles in your path, all work together so that you can become the person that God intended.

One of the superb reasons for developing self-confidence is that it is contagious; it propels and persuades others to feel confident as well. Joshua, the first official commanding general, proved that fact. The Hebrews had been wandering in the wilderness for forty years but when Joshua took command after the death of Moses, his first act was to assure the Hebrews that they would pass over the Jordan River and into the Promise Land in just three days. Of course, he did it. The word success is only found twice in the Bible and both mentions can be found in the book of Joshua.

Pay attention to the person that lacks confidence, he does not attract others or convince them of his worth because his mind is a negative force that repels rather than attract. Self-confidence can also dissolve inferiority. Did you ever think that spoken words of good could have such power? Did you know that affirming spoken words of good is more powerful than a thousand negative thoughts? Good is more—that's something to think about. If you can affirm a positive statement, you can overcome one thousand negative thoughts.

Building your confidence through your thoughts before going to sleep is a powerful way to develop self-confidence, which attracts powerful prosperity. Feed your mind confidence-filled thoughts as you drop of to sleep. If you fill your mind with happy, expectant thoughts of success, prosperity and good results, your subconscious will then take over those orders for you. During your sleep, your subconscious will obediently go to work to produce a prosperous tomorrow for you. You can gain control of each day the night before, by getting into the thought and mood of how you want tomorrow to unfold. Do not wait for others to assure you, praise you or express their confidence in you. Instead of fretting because they don't, assure yourself that someone cares, that The One who made you and who is ever interested in you is there to help.

To develop your innate self-confidence and your ability to succeed, I suggest using words of command. Affirmations release your self-confidence; speak your affirmations verbally at least five minutes a day, somewhere in private. At least once a day write out a favorite affirmation on success, confidence and perfect results fifteen times. By writing out words of confidence, you're helping to foster those ideas more fondly in your subconscious mind, which then works harder and faster to produce happier results. There are days when fear or doubts grip you when you may need to look at affirmations that you have written down on cards or in a book. You can even do this in the midst of a noisy atmosphere—ringing telephones or hectic activities—and no one ever needs to know that your booster shot comes from your prayers and affirmations.

Affirmations are your strongest confidence builders. When

doubt or fear impairs your ability to succeed, it seems to come upon you. My favorite one is: I can do all things through Christ whom strengthens me. I am strong in the Lord and in the power of His might, the perfect result now appears. I also like the following phrase: "Yea, though I walk through the valley of the shadow of death, I will fear no evil, for God is with me." Those words always make me feel better and can get me through anything.

These are just some of the affirmations that I use when things start going wrong or when something isn't necessarily going in the direction that I want. I just post my powerful affirmations around me and start repeating them over and over again. As I'm repeating it over and over again, God will show up and show out every time. From those affirmations, if I don't remember anything else, I can do all things in God who strengthens me. Do not forget the Lord's Prayer is a great confidence booster as it is filled with powerful affirmations.

The phrase "birds of a feather flock together" mean people associate with people of like minds. Another delightful way to develop self-confidence is to link yourself with self-confident people. You will suddenly begin to absorb their aura. Assurance will soon come alive by making contact with one or two success-minded, self-confident individuals. These types of people will subconsciously inspire you and lift you to higher levels of thought and expectation.

Perhaps Jesus was thinking of the power of self-confidence when he said, if I'd be lifted up I will draw all men unto me. (John 12:32) It's important to hang around people that we want to emulate. If you want to be confident, rich and prosperous, then hang around positive-minded people. If you want to be successful, associate yourself with successful people.

If you're hanging around people who are not self-confident, who are not going anywhere, you really need to wonder what you really think about yourself. Remember what you think about you bring about. Consequently, if you are hanging around people who aren't going anywhere, you must not be thinking about prosperous, successful and positive things.

I encourage you to consider one final way you can develop your own self-confidence, and help bring it forth in others— begin appreciating, praising, and calling forth the good in others. Speak confidently to others of their good points, dare to praise them, speak words of kindness, uplift and have confidence in a person while they're still struggling to succeed. Don't wait until the person has evidence of success. Don't wait until they've succeeded to slap them on the back, saying, "Girl, I'm proud of you. I knew you could do it the whole time." Praise their success even before their success occurs; that's when they really need to hear it. Most people wear a mask and if you can see behind the mask of their lives, you would realize what a tonic your kind words can often become. It's like throwing a life-line to a drowning person. It could be the turning point in his or her rise to success.

When whole-hearted confidence is expressed in yourself and in others, it has a miraculous power. Even the people the world considers highly successful crave words of confidence and thoughts of appreciation. You never know when a kind word can uplift a person.

I remember one time I had met a guy who started working at a company where I worked as the lead sales person, and for some reason he wasn't engaging. People didn't appreciate his energy. One day he came in my office and he said, "You think you something, don't you?" Knowing that he was having difficulties in his personal life, I simply looked at him and responded, "Why would you say that?" He went on to explain how he thought that I thought I was somebody. I said, "Well I am somebody. I'm God's child, just like you are." Then we started really talking and actually developed a wonderful working relationship. I started expressing kind words to him every day because my spirit told me to. Then I received a promotion to another office, so I didn't see him anymore. One day I called over to the other office because my spirit had been telling me to call him, only to discover that he hadn't been at work all week. The next call I placed was to his home to check up on him.

I could tell something was very wrong when he answered the phone; his voice was full of sadness. I began telling him that he was God's child and spoke words of encouragement hoping they would reach his soul. A week later he called and told me how thankful he was for my call that day because it reminded him of the God in himself. He confided that at the moment I called he had been sitting in his car about to end his own life. I am so grateful for listening to my inner spirit, even though I wish that I would have listened sooner before thoughts of suicide entered this man's mind. However, God is an on time God, and it all happened the way it was supposed to happen. You never know when words of kindness can change someone else's life.

Ultimately, as you walk your journey and meet people throughout your life, remember to send out prayers of love and praise to them. Your self-confidence will multiply; you'll never know just how much good your words of confidence can mean or how far they can go to produce good for others. This age-old truth applies that when you speak words of confidence concerning others you cannot help but attract it to yourself, since what you send out comes back to you multiplied. Remember, what you think about you bring about. More simply stated, what you put out in the world comes back to you. If you send out love, love comes back to you. Never be afraid to send love out, never be afraid to send words of kindness out.

Just your belief in others may be all they need to believe in themselves and to remind themselves that they are children of God. Prayer is the greatest confidence builder in the world. Through prayer, you tap into the Divine that releases great power in faith. Someone once said that the man who thinks he can is the one that succeeds.

Prayer is the most powerful thing we can do on this earth. Prayer is such a powerful energy, that it releases something magnificent. If your confidence is not where it needs to be, pray about it. If your life is not where you need it to be, pray about it. God just shows up and shows out when we put him first. Realize that God created us, and if we are trying to take it in our own hands to fix it, that's why it's broke. The very person, who created us, can create the life that we desire through us because God can't do any more for you than what he can do through you. Remember that all these things will come to help us step into our greatness, into who God created us to become.

When you are no longer afraid of hurt and failure and have stopped breathing life in your insecurities, then greatness can appear. When you find your rhythm, it becomes contagious and allows others to find their rhythm. Your liberation begins to liberate others. Your life speaks louder than you can ever scream or holler. You become such a presence that when you step in a room, your essence, your energy begins to permeate the air around you. People understand who you are, without you even having to explain yourself. They want to be around you and help you to accomplish your goals.

When you radiate your greatness, that comes back to you

1,000 fold. You become the magnet, drawing to you all that is great. Remember, however, that greatness isn't like a switch that comes on and stays on forever. You constantly have to choose to walk in your greatness because there are going to be times when you have to focus intently in order to make the highest choice. Every minute of every day you have the opportunity to choose to be powerful, good, humble, fearless, courageous and great—but it's all up to you. If you make the choice to be smaller than you are, just know that you always have another opportunity to choose again to step in your greatness.

Believe in you, love you, release the champion in you because when we release the champion in us, we're walking in the purpose that God has created for us. When we walk in the purpose God has created for us, we can't do anything other than live an amazing life even though sometimes it may get a little scary. Then you're ready to dance your dance, and sing your song, tell your story and set that inner champion free. You deserve to be happy; you deserve to be successful. You can choose to learn from your past and love your life. You can choose to rewrite the future and be okay with your past. This journey is to encourage and empower you to make choices, to build yourself up and experience happiness in your life today and every day; that's what this whole journey is about. It's learning to love yourself.

No, we can't rewrite the past. We can't change what happened in our past, but what we can do is learn lessons from those pasts and rewrite our whole story for the future. Today I dare you to rewrite your future. I dare you to write a future of stepping into your greatness, stepping into your purpose, living in your light living the way you were supposed to come and live on this earth. , I dare you today, just today, to rewrite your future.

Prayer

Father, I thank you for putting inside of me that seed of greatness. I thank you for allowing me to set my champion free. To allow me to walk in my light, walk in my purpose and walk in love. To liberate others and to give them permission to do the same, I thank you for that. I thank you for your words that you decreed in the Bible, I thank you for your word today. I thank you for allowing me and giving me the power to speak life into my own life and recognize that your presence lives inside of me every day, all the time, every where, no matter where I am and that I have the power to create my own future today.

I have the power to live an amazing life, if I just believe. Father, give me the faith today to change my life. Give me a clean heart and renew the right spirit inside of me today, Father. Today I ask you to open up the window and prepare a blessing so powerful beyond all blessings. Show up and show out in my life today, Father. Prepare a table of success, Father. I thank you for the love and support of everyone around me, the encouragement I thank you today,

Father. I thank you in the mighty name of Jesus, Amen.

Financial Prosperity

It's amazing what you can do when God is your business partner. Most people overlook that as a prosperity secret. Often, many people let riches pass them by because they do not ask the help of a Higher Power to learn how to obtain their good. Begin today to visualize your success, not just to become more prosperous, but to become independently wealthy.

The visualization process is two-fold: having the vision board and seeing it in your mind. When you can stop and take five minutes each day and create the world you want, you can attract your desires by seeing it in your world. Often you might not have the faith because you feel overwhelmed with life. It seems easier to settle for failure. Success requires work, consistency that you monitor your thoughts and your actions, checking to make sure that you are always in alignment with your goals and dreams.

Many people want to become financially independent, but they never make the grade due to lack of discipline. Concentrate on your prosperity. Believe and live as if you were already where you want to be today. For instance, you should begin your day by affirming greatness in your life, visualizing abundance, thinking prosperous thoughts first, as well as last, in your day. Stop and spend two minutes before starting your day by praying, affirming and decreeing things you want in your life. See the day going the way you want it to go—peaceful, harmonious, loving, etc. You should end your day by thanking

God and visualizing your life the next day.

When you can visualize daily, you can begin envisioning your financial independence for yourself and those you hold dear by filling your mind with pictures of the life you would like to lead, rather than being hypnotized by the mundane life you seem to be living at the moment. One of the ways to acquire the success you want is by becoming business partners with God. You do that by decreeing, creating a master plan, completing your vision board, and giving Him the space to make it happen. It may not happen overnight, yet it can and will happen if you dare to be persistent.

Envision and mentally accept the idea of financial independence for yourself and for all people. At first it may take some time or effort on your part to begin believing that success is possible for you, but the fruits of those efforts will make it much more prosperous with every thought. It's in every prosperous thought you hold, every vision entertained, every mental picture you have built. The Bible tells us we have not because we ask not. All you have to do is knock on the door using the tools that you have been given. It's really that simple.

Success is basically a personal goal for each one of us but that success may mean different things for different people. At one time in my life success meant that my children were successful; I was doing a successful job at being a parent. Now that they're about to transition into adulthood, my success goal is going to be totally different since the focus is now on me. We all need to really think about our goals and call attention to them in order to foster our own definition of financial independence and success. Ultimately, financial independence is what we all desire. Today is a day for financial independence, and we're claiming it!

God will open the door in ways that no human thought possible. We can just change our world just by believing, having the faith of a mustard seed. And we've seen it in our own lives and as well as the lives of others. I believe that President Barack Obama's going to do the same for what's going on in our world today. People inquired, how could he invest $50 billion into General Motors? What's going on here? But what people don't understand is President Barack is different because God's got his back. It was amazing the night that we were in downtown Chicago in Grant Park when he won the presidential nomination. It was the most peaceful gathering in Grant Park that I have ever witnessed. There were millions of people down there—blacks, whites, Asians, Latinos, East Indian—people of all ethnic groups sharing and caring. Even the notorious Chicago wind was silent. I know that God has President Barack's back no matter what challenges may lie ahead for him as he attempt to take into consideration the lives of all people, of big business and small business, of the young and the elderly. In my estimation, this has never before been accomplished by any of his predecessors in the White House.

We are the company we keep. You know, it's important that we share our dreams with people who believe in what we believe in. It's important to be around people who can encourage and uplift us. Birds of a feather flock together, right? If that holds true and you want to be successful, then it's time to hang around successful people. Begin to discipline yourself more, conserve your time and energy for what truly matters in your life. Associate only with other prosperous-minded people with whom you have compatible interests. As you turn from all that is unproductive or unrelated to your higher vision of prosperity, and as you stop trying to please others and dare to please the still small voice of progress within your own heart, you are well on your way to financial independence. Life is too short to hang around negative, critical, cynical, skeptical, judgmental, small-minded, jealous, dream-snatching people. Did I leave anyone out? Weed out all undesirable relationships. Be careful with whom and how you spend your time including your leisure time. You will discover a new way of life, you will be able to relax and really have fun because you have earned it. Unless you conserve and concentrate prior to that point, you will never attain your goals.

If you do not have a master plan for you life, create that world right now exactly how you want it to be and seek God's wisdom. It's important that you take five minutes out of each morning and thank God for your day and see your day being successful. It's important that you end your day with gratitude. When we send up the praises, God sends down the blessings. Become cognizant of the fact that you need to enthrall yourself in what it is that you're doing right now. So end your day with blessings, with being grateful for what God has given you through your families, through your jobs, through your financial situations.

My girlfriend, Marie, recently called to inform me that she was going through changes. She owns a business, for whatever reason, things were not going well for her. Contracts were being released from her and it impacted her business. She went to breakfast after services one Sunday and noticed these couples, these families, who come together every Sunday. She said from the looks of things—their dirty clothes, their unclean faces—they didn't have any money. She had wondered, God, where are they coming from? But then she noticed something else: they were always laughing and talking and having fun with each other. They just enjoyed each other's company. The so-called "well to do people" come, the ones driving the fancy cars with neatly pressed clothes, and they seem solemn and unhappy. She asked me, "What is it?" I replied, "It's because they were not making God their business partner. Just remember to make God your partner in your life, not just in your business and not just in your finances. Make God your business partner in your marriage." It should be you, your spouse and Him. Put God in your marriage. Put God in your parenting skills. Make God your partner in every area of your life—your career, your health, your personal relationships—God should be in the center of every relationship in your life.

Start thinking big, as most successful people do. They don't limit themselves; they think outside the box. If you desire to be free from limited thoughts and petty opinions, begin to think big. Concentrate on financial independence and you will lose the petty thinkers along the way. You will also cultivate enduring and satisfying friends that will help you climb the ladder of success. This point illustrates yet again that if you change your thoughts, you change your world. You don't have to tell people you don't want to be friends with them or that you're not going to be around. Once you start thinking differently, people who are not on your level will just move out of your way or they will want to rise to your level and learn what you're learning as well.

Dust off your dreams! If you have unfulfilled dreams and visions of greater prosperity and success tucked in the corner of your mind, don't keep them there any longer. Dare to bring them out and dust them off. Dare to think about the possibility of financial independence. Even at this point those long-lost dreams may seem impossible to fulfill, but when that

82

Janine A. Ingram

old defeating element of fear tries to creep up in your mind, saying there's no possible way for your financial independence to come true, tell yourself of the rich promises from the Bible.

I can't express how important it is to remind yourself to love you because no matter how many things you gain in this world from financial independence (that wonderful Mercedes, Lexus, Porsche, whatever) it doesn't mean anything if you're not loving yourself. It doesn't mean anything if you're not loving your family and giving love in your world. Love is a much more appealing concept than any material object you can have in this world. When you love yourself then you're giving from a rich vessel of love inside your heart. Remember, love is the key ingredient to all things. Even when you decide to embark on whatever business you desire or however you decide to create your financial independence, if you do it in love, I promise you the passion for it will be there and money will just start flowing in. There's an interesting thing about the fact that when you have a good attitude and when you have good feelings inside, you attract everything you need. When you feel good, you look good and you attract good. So remember to feel good about who you are, love who you are, just as you are right now—don't wait for the changes you think you need to make. Love yourself right now.

Prayer

Father I thank you this morning for all things. Thank you for giving me the understanding of the steps to take in order to manifest goodness in my life, Father. Thank you for the opportunity to seek your wisdom today and every day. Thank you for the opportunity to learn of the wisdom of Christ inside of me, so I can understand how to manifest the Christ Consciousness and allowing my presence to be a blessing. Thank you today for decreeing all goodness in my life. Thank you today for demanding and understanding that all I have to do is ask. All I need to manage is the faith of a mustard seed.

Thank you for the simple things in life. Thank you for bestowing your goodness in my life and teaching me, through your word that I can have all things—wonderful children, amazing friends, a loving family, a prosperous life and, more importantly, phenomenal relationships including one with myself. I thank you for all those things. I thank you for teaching me that to live a wealthy and prosperous life means to live a holistic life; that it's about more than just having money, more than having material possessions, but enjoying a peaceful, harmonious life and all other things will follow.

And so it is.

Power Through Collective Prayer: The Prayer Line

God is an awesome God. God is an amazing God. I am the host of a call-in conference line known as the Prayer Line which is a very interesting story. My friend, Nicole Jones, owner of Sensual Steps and author of "Dare to Walk in My Shoes" is an absolutely amazing woman. If you know anything about Nikki, she does not take no for an answer. The Prayer Line started when life took a series of turns for my friend. She was experiencing some challenges, and prayer and affirmation was the only way change was going to occur.

As I assisted her in raising her consciousness, she began to see the rebirth quickly. She was so excited she wanted to share the knowledge I had shared with her with others. Now Nikki is a person who is strong, confident, persistent, strong-willed and, as I mentioned above, does not take no for an answer. I love her dearly, but I have to say she was a bulldog when trying to convince me that I needed to start a prayer line. I kept telling her no, and she kept trying to explain why I needed to do this line. Now me being me, I could not see myself on a prayer line facilitating a prayer group. I do know people have always looked to me for inspiration; even sometimes for answers to their questions. The reason for this is primarily because they saw me with an unshakeable type of faith, but even more important, with a peace that surpassed their understanding.

Maybe that perception was true. I honestly did not believe I was qualified to lead a prayer group.

I never used to pray out loud or speak in front of people without sweating and having butterflies in my stomach. I actually felt that Nikki was a better fit for the facilitator of such a group. Nikki loves the microphone. She loves to talk and can speak for hours. I even explained why I thought she should be the one to run this group. Of course, she did not think she was the one for the job.

I called my friend Myra and explained what Nikki was trying to convince me to do. Now she really blew me out of the water because she agreed! I could not believe she thought I was capable of doing a prayer line, but I promised her I would think about it. Meanwhile, Nikki was not letting up on this idea. She decided to have her girl, Tiffany, call me. Tiffany decided to pull out the God card. She reminded me of the reason God put people in our lives to help us grow. Between the three of them, they were starting to wear me down.

Nikki pulled out all her cards and was not letting go. All I could think was what Moses was thinking when God told him to go to Egypt and tell the powers that be to let his people go. Moses felt Aaron was a better speaker like I felt Nikki was better for this job. But as life would have it, I finally decided to do the prayer line.

We started out with ten people on the phone praying together and reading inspirational books as well as the Bible. We even started doing little get together's to facilitate different classes. For example, we had a 5:00 a.m. morning sunrise service where we prayed, watched the sunrise; wrote letters of things we wanted to release from our lives and burned them in a fire we started on the lake. It was so beautiful. After the release ceremony we wrote love letters to ourselves. It was a very cleansing experience. After the ceremony we dined together on the lake. I had tables with white tablecloths and gold candles with gold and white accessories.

I also facilitated other classes such as a phenomenal vision board class. It has been six months since the Prayer Line began, and there was anywhere from 70 to 80 people on the phone from different states at one time. I guess Nikki knew what she was talking about. I can honestly say the Prayer Line has been a blessing to me. I have grown tremendously, not to mention I have learned a lot. I have developed more speaking confidence as I have increased knowledge to share with others. I am grateful that God brings people in your life to see the things you do not want to see or cannot see.

There are amazing things that occur with callers all the time. For example, there was one caller who was in foreclosure. She actually had the sheriff date and was packing her stuff up and her baby's things. She was praying for God's will to be done, and we were praying on the prayer line for her abundance as well. Do you know what happened? She called the bank to see by what date she would need to be out of her house, but the bank informed her that they had stopped the foreclosure proceedings and that someone would call her back with additional information. She received a call back from her bank the same day, and they told her that they would rework things so she could have the ability to remain in her home—and she's still in her house today. We just have to learn to allow God to work through us.

Proverbs 3:56 says "Trust in the Lord with all thine heart and lean not unto thine own understanding. In all thy ways acknowledge Him and He shall direct they path." It doesn't say trust in your ability to pay or trust in your own ability. It doesn't say trust in where you think the money or resources should come from. It says to trust in God, trust in me, trust in the Father. "And in all thy ways acknowledge him and he shall direct thy path." It doesn't say just give me a few things in your life or God will just handle the basic things. God will handle everything in your life; even the debt, that health challenge, our children and that troubled marriage.

You have to understand that God is bigger than what we believe. I'm telling you this from experience and not from just talking the talk. Most people who've been on the prayer line since we studied the *Dynamic Laws of Prosperity* together know that God is amazing just by the testimonies that came out in just a short while on those phone calls.

Most people don't understand how to pray. People think we get on our knees and start praying and asking, pleading, or begging God. That doesn't move God; faith moves God. Faith and limiting thoughts can't exist in the same space. When you put your desire out there, just ask God to give the date and truly put it in His hand. Every time you try to take it out of God's hand, remember your affirmations.

When I felt weak about things going on in my life, sometimes I would go to the park and scream my affirmations out loud; sometimes I would scream the Our Father prayer out loud. Folks might have thought I was a little off balance, but that didn't matter to me. Everything I had in my heart came into fruition. Many people come up to me and say, "You must be a millionaire." There was even a time when people asked if I sold drugs. Absolutely not! I have faith.

Sometimes you will have unexpected miracles happen in your life. Sometimes God will have people walk up to you and give you things or information that lead to the very thing you desire. Someone will just walk up to you and give you a check at the time you need it most. You'll have an investor come up and tell you that God told them to assist you with one thing or another.

I've been going to Intender's Circle once a week. Intender Circle is a group of like mind people coming together to speak what we are grateful for, then speak what we intend to manifest in our lives. Everyone in the group aligns (one spirit one mind) with your intention, and gives them power. One of the ladies told the story of a woman who was in the midst of getting put out of her home because both she and her husband had lost their jobs. This man saw the sheriff's men putting her furniture and the rest of her belongings out into the street. He walked up and asked her what was going on. Minutes later he wrote a check in the amount necessary to return her house to her possession. He paid off her house, paid up her bills and she is still living in her house today.

I heard a similar story of a woman in California who was in foreclosure. She was sitting on the steps of her porch, crying, as the sheriff sale was taking place inside. One of the potential buyers was about to step inside, but walked past the woman and asked why she was crying. The woman explained her circumstances and guess what? That lady, a total stranger to the woman, went inside and bought her house back and gave her the house. They call the woman "the foreclosure angel." These stories serve as a reminder of how awesome God is. He's bigger than our own limited thoughts.

When you write down your bills and they total up to $10,000, $20,000, $100,000 $500,000—that's nothing to God. It may seem like an enormous amount of money to you, but it's nothing to God. Don't fall into the thought process of, "Whew! I think I owe a whole lot of money. There's no way I can manifest that much." Again, you leave this to God. Give thanks for the immediate and complete payments of all financial obligations; quickly and in peace, and you leave the rest to God. When the bill collectors call, don't waver in your belief. There have been times when bill collectors have called my home, and I told them straight up, "I don't know when I'm going to pay you but I do know God is going to pay you."

Don't be afraid to talk to your bill collectors and tell them I know God's going to give me the money to pay. And no matter what they say, just tell them what your spirit tells you to say. I didn't run from my bill collectors because I knew God was going to give me whatever I needed. I know sometimes I sounded like a fool to them. Sometimes I would even laugh at myself. God is big enough to pay all your debts. God is big enough to pay all $500,000 worth of debt. God is big enough to pay $1,000,000 in IRS debt. We have to have faith because God only operates in faith.

When negative thoughts come into your mind and try to knock you off your feet, you have to believe in your affirmations. The reason we decree our visions into existence is because there's power in the tongue. There's power in the spoken word. It will shift the paradigm of your thoughts, of your world. There were times I've walked in places where the people said they were not going to take a meeting with me. I said, I can do all things in Christ who strengthens me. I would just say it over and over again. I can do all things in Christ who strengthens me. I can do all things in Christ who strengthens me. People will go out of their way to help you, and they won't even know why. It's not you; it's the God in you. It's the spirit in them and God is working through them to help you.

You know you have to be bold about God. You have to be courageous. If you remember when Jesus decided who he would choose as his disciples, he didn't choose any passive people who would say, "Okay, well, I don't know how God's going to work this out." No! He chose bold people, who would use their energy in the right, positive direction.

Paul was bold. In our time he would've been considered a straight up gangsta. He was beating people up, charging people usury rates and doing all kinds of things that were not Christ-like. But God saw the boldness in him. God knew he needed warriors; that he needed people who were going to have faith beyond all understanding. And that's what this is all about—being warriors. It's about putting that spiritual armor on, using spiritual tools and having faith beyond all understanding.

His word say we can speak, we can decree, we can ask. This is not Janine Ingram's word, but I'm telling you as a living example what God can do for us. Whatever issue you believe is too big for God; I want you to put it in God's hand today. And if you put that date on there and everything doesn't come together by the time you need it to, remember our time and spiritual time isn't always the same. Just change to a new date God is still in the process of working things out. As your faith gets stronger and you elevate your consciousness, the easier you will manifest and demonstrate God's word in your life.

My grandmother used to say something really interesting: when you find yourself in a problem, you have to see your way through it. Now I didn't really understand what she meant by that when I was younger, but with the knowledge I have today it means for me to mentally see in my mind that God is fixing the problem. That's another powerful tool.

Allow God's will to work in your life. In your meditations, ask for God's will to come through you. We're so used to being in control. Some of us are CEO's of companies, some of us run a household and businesses, and some of us supervise and manage others; so we think we have to live our lives always in control. We have to remember that God is ultimately in control.

God can restore marriages. God can restore that million dollars that seemed to disappear into thin air. He can restore that money that you may owe to the IRS or whoever else you owe. God can heal your bank account. God can restore your body weight if you just believe and you can see it in your mind. God can heal the sick. God can heal your body image, but you have to have faith. And the interesting thing about it is we don't even have to have a whole lot of faith, just the faith of a mustard seed.

Prayer

I thank you for the immediate and complete payment of all financial obligations. I'm asking you in the mighty name of Jesus to heal my finances. I'm asking you to do your will in my financial obligations. Teach me to lean not to my own understanding. Teach me to release limited thoughts and to understand the vastness of who you are.

Thank you for being such an awesome God. Thank you for being an amazing God. Thank you for the opportunity to express your will being done through my life today. Thank you for using me as a vessel today. Thank you for using me to manifest that Christ Consciousness.

Alternative Prayer

Thank you for the opportunity to heal the mental processes that I need to heal so that I can move on to understand how to shift my paradigm, Father. Thank you for your will being so simple in my life. Thank you for teaching me how to use my spiritual armor and tools to decree and declare your word in my life. Thank you for being such a great Creator, creating wonderful things through me and using me in a mighty way. Thank you for using me in so many ways I can't even understand.

I thank you for feeling your presence. I thank you for the powerful wisdom of our ancestors. I thank you for the powerful wisdom of the elderly. I thank you for the powerful wisdom that comes through from family and total strangers. I thank you because you're an awesome God. I'm just grateful for being able to allow you to work in my life easy and effortlessly. I'm just grateful for understanding that I don't have to worry, that I don't have to stress, that all I have to do is speak the word and know that all things will come together in God.

I'm thankful for the opportunity for people to come together and give their stories and remind us of how awesome you are, Father. Thank you, thank you in the mighty name of Jesus for showing up and showing out in everybody's life today. I ask you to give them the desires of their heart, Father. I'm asking you to manifest blessings beyond understanding. I'm asking you to do some amazing results, Father. I'm asking you to show them how speaking words into existence will be the right way to go. I'm asking you to show them that your word is the truth.

As you go before them today and prepare the table of success, I ask that you give them peace today. Give them joy and happiness today. I ask you to give them strength, wisdom and courage to do your will today. And I'm asking you to give them a joyful day today, to just rejoice in your name today, Father; to just be grateful and joyful today. Just let it be a peaceful, harmonious day and that there will be peace across the world, peace in every household, peace in the workplace, peace on the bus, peace driving to work, peace riding the train, peace up in the airplanes.

Amen

Prayer for the People on the Prayer Line

We thank you for every person under this prayer line today. We thank you for the collective energy. We thank you for the individual goals and thank you for the desires of each and every person on these calls, Father. We just thank you for showing up and showing out in each and every one of our lives today. Father, you're an awesome God. And we thank you for being so awesome.

Amen

Father as I move on this journey I ask you to teach me how to have that one-on-one personal relationship with you. I'm asking you to reveal the mysteries of life to me in my meditations, as I become still and know that you are God—knowing that the I Am that I Am presence exists in everything that I do. That the Great I Am presence exist inside of me. And Father thank you for creating angels to protect me. You've given me master guides and the benefit of the wisdom of the ancestors. You said all I have to do is seek your wisdom and I can have all the abundance and benefits to live this life and walk this journey. I don't have to wonder, all I have to do is lean to you. I ask that you hear my prayers. And I thank you for answered prayer.

And so it is, and so it is.

Father, thank you for the opportunity for prayer and meditation. Father, thank you for the power of collective energy, to encourage and uplift and bring forth the manifestation of our Christ consciousness, we thank you father for that. Father, we thank you in the mighty name of Jesus, for the earth, the sun, the rain, the flowers, the trees, the moon. Father, we just thank you for so many blessings that you have bestowed upon our life.

We thank you for each and every one of our individual talents that we bring to the table. We thank you for each one of us being unique. We thank you for allowing us to live on purpose, we thank you for allowing us to walk this spiritual journey in finding the reason why you put us on this earth, that purpose gave life to us. We thank you for how you just orderly orchestrated our lives so that we can create the life that we desire so that we can live an amazing, abundant, rich, loved and charm-filled life. We just thank you in the mighty name of Jesus for all of our blessings.

Thank you. Amen.

Cherish the Wealth

Wealth, power, health, happiness and fulfillment depend on one person . . . yourself. This book alone will not bring you these characteristics. But if these things are what you desire, this book will stimulate you to develop unlimited powers that exist in each and every one of us. Good health and happiness can be yours. Wealth—you can acquire it. Power—you have it in unlimited quantities within you. But you must decide whether you are willing to put in the work to extract and use the success principles outlined in this book. The choice is yours and yours alone. We must be persistent in our endeavors for success, especially since now we have read this book "Born to be Rich" and understand that prosperity is our Divine right. We should persist in claiming it!!! We must be bold, daring and fearless. We should not hesitate, we should go after what we want until we get the results we desire.

The Creator of all things gave you complete, unchallengeable dominion over one thing for sure, and that is your mind . . . your thoughts. Your mental attitude gives your personality a drawing power to attract your most dominate thoughts whether good or bad. Your capacity to believe is your greatest most powerful potential asset. Your mental attitude is the medium by which you attract what you desire.

How do we cherish or maintain that wealth we created? By remembering the steps it took to get there. That same "in it to win it and keep it" attitude. That same powerful energy of affirming, visualizing and writing the vision down. We must always remember to keep an attitude of gratitude. When you give thanks or praise around a situation, you are invoking Divine favor which is then released to produce exciting results. Bless a thing or a person then it will bless you! Curse a person or thing and it will curse you! To bless means to bring forth good in a situation or personality. The more you praise the presence of God in you, the better you receive. Praise multiplies goodness. Praise multiplies blessings. The more you give praise the more you will have to give thanks and praise for. You will become like David, who kept praising God, and God kept on blessing him and pouring out so many blessings on David until one day he shouted "My cup runneth over!" (Psalms 23:5) We, too, should praise God and be thankful like David so one day we can shout, "Lord, my cup runneth over!" Through the presence and power of God in you, you can make every day a new beginning toward a more prosperous, more dynamic, more joyful way of life.

Our Heavenly Father is longing to be good to you! The word tells us "Fear not, little flock, for it is your father's good pleasure to give you the desire's of the heart." He even wants to give you the secret dreams inside of your heart. The Universe is amazing; God is amazing! We just need only to believe His command and decree those things as if they were so! It shall be done!

TAKE THE LIMITS OFF GOD TODAY! DREAM THESE GOD-SIZE DREAMS! LET THE GOD TIMES ROLL!

And so it is.

Testimonials

Nicole Jones

Last year appeared to have been one of the most difficult years of my life. At a second glance, 2009 was pretty tough, but it also turned out to be one of the best years of my life. Please allow me to briefly explain why: I was broken; everything in my life was turned upside down. I was going through a divorce, financial strife, losing my business and having severe relationship issues with a few people that were once close to me.

I can remember asking God to remove all things that were not of Him from my life. Boy I didn't know what I was in for asking this request. Janine Ingram, my very good friend and spiritual mentor, helped work with me during each of these difficult stages. She said, "You must affirm greatness back into your life."

In between my constant pity parties I began to rekindle my faith in the Lord and practice the teachings of affirmation, forgiveness and believing in the infinite possibilities for my life. Miracle after miracle began to manifest. My business became restored; a new love entered into my life, financial strife began to turn into financial prosperity. My faith escalated to a level that I never even knew existed before.

One word that inspires me and encourages me daily is the simple yet powerful word...BELIEVE.

Michelle Mason

August 2009, I hit rock bottom. Every aspect of my life was in chaos. In my anger at God, I decided that maybe my journey should end because the path was rugged. It hurt to even breathe. I was already dead inside; my spirit was lifeless.

Moments before ending my life, I reached out to a friend. In a calm voice my friend asked, "Why would you do that?"

I had many reasons, all which made sense to me at the time. In her reflections from what she had learned along the way of her spiritual journey and life experiences, she shared things that touched my heart. "You need to fix you. This pain that you feel is deeply rooted."

At the time, I would have preferred swallowing the waters of Lake Michigan to doing what she asked. But I drank in the information that was being given to me and continued to listen. I was encouraged to have a personal talk with Janine, and I did. She didn't stand in judgment of me. Instead, she helped to remove the dead layers of baggage that were burying me in a literal since. As she fed my spirit, I decided that I wanted more . . . more for me.

I joined the prayer line and, for once in a long time, I felt alive again. I found that among me there were others that were going through tough times, gaining wisdom, elevating themselves and others, creating vision boards, practicing lessons within the Dynamic Laws of Prosperity and establishing positive peer relationships with individuals that wanted to be prosperous in every area of their being. Thank God for allowing Janine into my life, for that was the lifeline that I caught at the end of my wave.

Today, I have a better relationship with God, myself, family and friends. I've been blessed professionally and have been placed in a position to bless others. Many amazing things continue to happen and I'm excited!!!

Stacie Spears

I am a person that attends church on Sunday and bible study on Wednesday every week. Because of the struggles of these trying times, I was in need of so much more. I was introduced to the prayer line to supplement what I was acquiring at church. I am so thankful for the women that decided that there should be a means for people all over the world to be able to begin every weekday with a word from God, which led to the birth of the Divine Connection prayer line.

Janine is a phenomenal woman that facilitates the call each day. She is one of the most powerful prayer warriors that I have had the pleasure of praying with since I began my intensive journey with the Lord. Anyone that has ever spoken to Janine can attest to the fact that she is truly one of the anointed chosen by God. Janine has been blessed with a tremendous gift. She provides thought-provoking lessons on a daily basis that are inspirational and motivational.

During the call there is time set aside for affirmations that are said in unity. The affirming portion of the call has affected my entire household in such an amazing way that even my 6-year-old twins are praying, affirming and decreeing nothing but prosperity in their own little lives each day. I am so thankful that I am able to teach my children the right way to begin their day.

Janine not only leads prayer with the group, but she also remains on the call until every need of every person has been addressed. With all of that, she does not stop there. Janine extends the courtesy for anyone to call her at any time, day or night, to pray, talk and to be uplifted in their time of need. I have been one of the people that have had to rely on her outside of the call on numerous occasions. It has touched my heart beyond any measure to know that there is a woman that has never met many of the callers personally, and yet she still offers unconditional love and understanding.

Every encounter that I have had with Janine has left me better than I had been before. Since I began being on the call, I have had so many of my loved ones tell me how I have changed. I have been seeing life in a much more positive way. As a result, I have been experiencing more blessings and prosperity.

Janine is a compassionate woman that will lift the lowest person to levels that they could have possibly never dreamed of attaining. I would recommend that everyone experience the gift that God has given Janine to minister and spread the word of the Lord, prosperity, peace and love.

Beatrix Davis

I met Janine Ingram in the lateral part of 2009. Our introduction was by a mutual friend that I've known for more than 5 years. It was strange because the length of time I have known Mrs. Knox our paths had not crossed. Nevertheless, it just confirmed that God gives you what you need when you need it. Janine entered my life at a very pivotal point; I was in battle with life itself between destruction and survival. My family suffered a major loss in July 2008: the life of my mother-in-law was called home. The following year, in April of 2009, my father surrendered to a three-year battle with cancer and my mother moved on to her next life in July 2009. My marriage was not weathering the storm. If I had to describe my state of being in one word, it would be PAIN!!!! I lived in it every second of the day; I carried it in my heart, on my mind and in the mere depth of my soul. Let me just ask you, do you know what it feels like to awake every morning and suit up for battle in war with your emotional you? That is a mild description of where I was in life when God sent "My Very Own Personal Angel."

Janine's spirit is so unique; she beholds within her the ability to save the world. Her warm and very gentle spirit embodies you upon immediate contact. Her smile relieves you and lets you know that it is going to be all right. We are blessed that Nicole Jones convinced her to share her faith and glory of God with us every morning on the prayer line. The birth of this line has been a blessing in itself to many people. However, for me it has been a rebirth of my faith, a restoration of my relationship with God and a recreation of my vision. In a very short period, Janine's profound guidance, strength, wisdom and education of living life to the fullest with God's blessing regenerated my life and pure existence.

Mirion Green

The reason evil runs rampant is because a few good men remain silent. The reason some people do not hear the blessed voices of others are because a few good men remain silent. Well, Janine Ingram is the best kept secret in which we should not remain silent. Janine is loving, patient and understanding. She has an anointing on her life so strong that when you are in her presence you also feel the presence of God.

Everyone says Janine sees things through rose-colored glasses; she sees the good in everyone and sees the positive in every situation. Janine truly believes in the power of prayer, and she is always so willing to pray you out of a situation. She has so much faith that you would believe your circumstances are solved based on her faith. Janine is like that sunshine and brisk wind after a stormy, hot day; she is such an inspiration to all of her family and friends.

If I had the time, I would tell you how Janine has always walked with boldness. If I had the time, I would tell you how Janine has always walked with integrity and respect. If I had the time, I would tell you how Janine doesn't just talk but she practices what she preaches. If I had the time, I would tell you how Janine is like a palm tree in the midst of a storm. If I had the time, I would go on forever about the blessing God has given us with giving us Janine.

I thank God for Janine and allowing God to use her in such a mighty way, and I believe through her obedience she will reach and change the lives of millions. Janine is such a powerful woman of God.

Deborah Gary

The morning call has been the most instrumental tool for me in the past year in my growth of knowledge in my purpose in life and many other areas. The same week I began the call, my blessings began to literally shower my world. God reacts to faith and, to tell the truth, I became addicted to waking up and making the call like someone is addicted to coffee. I began to feel like I could not face my day without it. But then on the mornings there was no call, I still got up and began to pray on my own and say my affirmations while sometimes journaling and/or meditating all of which I learned from the morning call. I never did these things before on my own.

I am a better mother, wife, friend, sister, daughter, co-worker, businesswoman and servant of God now. I have less stress, more peace, joy, and understanding of God and his plan for me. I am ecstatic when I've invited others on the call, and they are equally blessed if not more. For me the call is life changing for the better and I am so thankful that Janine has allowed God to work through her to facilitate it.

Myra Neal

I joined the Prayer Connection in May '09. I honestly can say I had no strong expectations for myself other than communing with my friends daily, thinking prosperous thoughts and creating a positive attitude. The discipline it would take waking at 6:00 a.m. each morning committing myself to praying and prospering with friends would be the reward.

Six months later I cannot imagine starting my day without it. It's more than a Sunday church service once a week. It's a daily inspiration, motivating the gathering of like minds raising our consciousness and praises to the Lord.

As we gather each morning I am held in constant awe as the messages flowing through and to Janine from the Lord. The Lord uses her soul to deliver our daily bread in a fresh new perspective called enrichment for the soul; it's food you can use. The method of using our life energies to create our wealth, health and happiness is new to me. Since I have embraced the concept, I find this completely life changing for me. My faith, attitude and confidence to face challenges in my life has grown expeditiously over these months.

Some may initially come for curiosity or the novelty of it all. But many stay because it is literally LIFE CHANGING!

Lovie Bernard

When I joined the prayer line in September of 2009, I was at a low point. I didn't like myself very much, and I didn't feel like I had time to dream. At 58, I felt like my best days were gone. My hope had been shattered, and I didn't feel I had a lot to look forward to. Making that call was the best thing that happened to me. Meeting Janine has changed my life.

The first thing she taught me is my life is not defined by man. God is in control, and he is the first and he is the last. As long as God's on your side, it's a done deal. The people on the prayer line all have something they're trying to change or someplace they're trying to go. I am so blessed to be with such an encouraging group even though some of us only know each other by voices. The love radiates and permeates deep in to your soul. From Janine's vision and her love and trust in us and for us we know where we're going. And thru the grace of God may we grab someone else and take them on the journey with us.

I love you, Janine. Keep on doing God's work, and we'll keep on lifting you up. We'll succeed one person at a time.

Nelson Dax

Lovie Bernard and I were co-workers at the Chicago Mercantile Exchange for many years. But with mergers and acquisitions, layoffs and downsizing, we both were released years apart and lost contact. One day a mutual friend gave me the news that Lovie was having a bout with cancer and gave me her phone number. I called her, and we became reconnected and even became business partners. Lovie has always had a caring spirit and, even with her own pressing issues, she still was more concerned about others. In a conversation about how she keeps her spirits up she mentioned the name Janine Ingram and that she has a prayer conference call every morning at 6:00 a.m. "you need to get on that call." I acknowledged I would and after more invites I finally did.

It was amazing! The spirit of this voice coming over the phone line was so motivating, so uplifting it had to be another way God had decided to speak to me. I listened for a couple of months and finally the day came when I was able to put a visual to the voice. It only added more excitement to me committing to this call every morning. I finally began to understand the story behind her and Nicole Jones agreeing that this woman of God had to find a vehicle to spread her spirit and God's word to as many as will receive it. It is with that motivation that I began a group page on Facebook called "The Source" because as she has taught and reminded us every morning "God is the source of my unlimited supply. Everything and everybody prospers me now."

I acknowledge that my spiritual journey and uplifted spirit I have is because of the manifestation of more prayer in my life that starts everyday at 6:00 a.m. It has blessed me in so many ways which include confidence, personal development and improved relationships. All I can say is thank you Lord for again ordering my steps. Thank you Janine Ingram for the lessons of life you speak to me every morning and, with much love and gratitude, thank you Lovie Bernard for allowing God to use you.

Sister Colette Grant

Janine Ingram is a phenomenal woman. She is a blessing to know. She is truly a servant or a channel through which God uses. She facilitates a prayer connection call in the early hours of the morning where people from all over the country come on the telephone to give honor to the presence of God and to hear her give a Bible verse or tell an amazing story about the miracles of Jesus. Thank you, Janine, for saying yes!

I have always recognized a spiritual presence in the world and something or someone bigger than me was ordering my steps. In my spiritual walk, I remember the most interesting bible study class I attended called "God Speaks." It basically opened my eyes to the many different ways that God speaks to me. It included the obvious, Pastors and teachers, but also strangers and many other signs. I believe this best defines that latest chapter in my life and my introduction to Janine Ingram.

Reverend Larry Q. Clemmons
—Just for the Record

It was in the spring of 1999 that I began to see small tumors appear around my arms, neck and legs. At first they would come and stay visible for about a week and then disappear. By August of the same year the tumors began to stay longer. I contacted a well-known dermatologist in Chicago named Dr. James Fisher. He took a sample of tissue of three of the tumors and submitted them for biopsy. The pathology came back after careful study that determined that I had Lymphoma. Dr. Fisher said that based on the report I had less than a 15% chance of survival even with extreme chemotherapy and/or radiation. My day was dying and my cousin had been diagnosed with breast cancer and headed for surgery and chemotherapy. All this took place in September of 1999.

I did not want to talk about this with anyone and only my wife knew about it. I was being prayerful and quiet. One day a friend going back about 40 years called me. We hadn't talked in months. She said that she felt something was wrong and wanted me to share it with her. I told her that my main concern was my cousin with breast cancer. My friend Collette insisted that her concern was about me, but I continued to focus on my cousin.

Collette then told me about two incidents that happened to her. While in a parking lot waiting for her daughter who was in a dentist appointment, Collette was reading in her car with the window open drinking a bottle of juice. Not looking, she went to take a sip and a bee that had landed on the rim of the bottle stung her on the tongue. Collette is allergic to bee stings. She was fearful that because of the swelling, she would be unable to breath. Her tongue was swelling more every second, and Collette was uncertain that she could get to a hospital in time. There was also the issue of leaving her daughter with no way of letting her know what was happening. Collette said that these words came to her mind; "I am made in the image and likeness of God. God is whole, perfect and complete. What is true about God is true about me."

As she continued to repeat these words over and over again the swelling decreased and within minutes she was back to normal. A few weeks later she said to me, while ironing some clothes she broke out with itchy bumps. She could hardly contain herself. Then the healing words came back to her. She repeated them over and over as before, and within a few minutes the itching and the bumps went away. Collette went on to say that she believed that those two incidents and the spiritual utterances that God revealed to her were for my benefit.

I could not believe what I was hearing. Without her knowing anything about my condition, God had prepared her to reveal to me the answer to my prayer, a prayer for healing and restoration. After hearing this, I told Collette my whole story. I thanked her for listening and doing the will of God. I prayed using the spiritual utterances that were given to Collette and within three months all the tumors were gone. My dermatologist and my internist were amazed. The internist questioned the accuracy of the pathology report, but was assured that the findings were accurate, thorough and complete. To this day, now ten years later, my doctors are still in amazement.

I am grateful to Collette. I praise God and exalt his name. I exalt his love, his mercy, his grace and his peace. I endeavor to lift him up by living in harmony with his will and purpose. God made me in his image and likeness to be a reflection of his presence in my daily walk. I am not here just to serve God, but to be his expressed image here on Earth. God has asked me to do five things: I am to love God above all things, love my neighbor as I love myself, love my enemies, forgive and refrain from judgment. My testimony is to let people know that God is present and doing great works now just as God has done in the past. The greater message for me to share with the world is that we are all made in the image and likeness of God. Our attention should be on living the truth. The human condition will never be perfect.

Perfection is realized in recognizing our oneness with the Spirit of God.

Pia Washington
—*Thank you from California!*

I am writing this thank you email because I do not have your mailing address for a thank you card! I have been so BLESSED by the call each and every day since my best friend Stacie invited me to join. It has been interesting to see how God has been "showing up" in my life to let me know it is worth getting up before 4:00 a.m. to participate in praising him.

I didn't get a chance to testify this morning on the call, but I wanted to let you know that on Wednesday, Day 1 of the 21 day journey, you quoted the same scripture I had just been reading the day before. You mentioned the woman with the issue of blood and my oldest son has sickle cell disease. He is a smart, funny and handsome young man and has been fairly healthy. But on Sunday night he went into a pain crisis in both of his arms. Not only could he not go to work, but he was having a hard time feeding himself (he is 20 years old). Usually his crises last for about a week or longer, and sometimes he is even hospitalized and put on morphine for the pain—but not this time. I truly believe in the power of many people touching and agreeing and even though you didn't know my situation and you were praying healing over someone else, it was still heard by God. By Wednesday night, his pain was gone and he returned to work on Thursday morning.

I really appreciate you so much and I know that God will continue to bless you in many ways.

Tammy Oliver

I am writing this letter to express how much Janine Ingram and the conference call she holds every morning has completely transformed my life. I joined the called for the first time in September of 2009. My sister, Paula Greene, invited me to join the call because I was at the lowest point in my life. In September 2009 I was experiencing hardship in every aspect of my life. I was bitter, doubtful, angry and ready to give up on everything that was against me.

After one week on the call, Janine taught a lesson on forgiveness. That began my transformation. The examples she gave and Bible verses she referenced caused me to read my Bible more to gain understanding. The affirmations on forgiveness and writing in my journal helped me to release my anger. Immediately things began to shift and change in my life, so much so this letter would be pages long if I attempted to write every testimony.

I am so happy that Janine would take time out of her personal life for people she doesn't even know that are on the call. Many times I have called her in tears. Once our conversation is over I've felt things were going to change for the better if I followed her directions. She is so dedicated to so many strangers and helping us all to improve of lives and our future.

I just can not say enough about how positive this experience has been for me. It is by far the greatest thing that has happened. It was just what I needed at that exact moment. Needless to say, my story is far from over. As of today my son is on the honor roll at one of the greatest schools in Chicago. My business is weeks away from opening, and I have received thousands of dollars from people I barely even know. I can't begin to thank Janine enough for praying with me and helping to see the good in myself as well as others. Be blessed!

Rena Fraiser

Giving God the honor, glory, thanks and the praise; I ask that he continues to make a way for everyone, especially my family. I am a new pray line participant with three weeks of participation. I was invited by one of my great friends.

Ironically, the morning I joined the prayer line I took my 4-year-old son to the bathroom and began pondering how I could be a vessel to demonstrate greater love for everyone, especially my family members as I have not exactly been a good beacon for this act with them yet seem to exhibit it greatly with friends. Why is that? Hence, I meditated with myself and God and picked up the phone and dialed into the call as I quickly realized I had to begin somewhere; I simply had to make the effort to begin. You have to want to change your situation for yourself.

I say to you right now, I am in a season of great worry in my life regarding my finances as I have lost my job. Feverishly, I am working hard to keep my home over my children's heads, pay my bills, keep the car in the garage and grow both of my new businesses while focusing on getting them up and running. I desperately need financial resources and/or pro bono resources, among other things. Needless to say, I am doing a lot of soul searching, God searching, healing, getting to know my father

Jesus Christ on a more personal level and becoming a better, more prosperous child of God for my children and their future. This is not something I am doing out of my circumstances but because of my circumstances . . . it's a necessity. I need to have a better relationship with God. A relationship that began during my childhood that has somewhat escaped me throughout adulthood.

As God teaches us that we should not worry because just as surely as he provides for the lilies that feed off the earth he will provide for us as he loves us more. This is a hard and difficult lesson. However, I am trusting God all the way, renewing my faith and releasing my worries to him, although it is an ongoing every day battle that I seek God in every second of the day! My biggest challenges are the fear of losing everything, forgiveness and always thinking in a positive attitude, discarding any and all negative words and thoughts.

My goal for myself and my family during this journey is to read the Bible and communicate with God on a daily level. The prayer call is an exceptional way to begin my day. I must say, it took me a week to get adjusted to just rolling over and calling; but I tell you I need God in every way imaginable to rain down his effervescence on my soul so I might have a closer, personal walk with him and engage my children in the same.

Since joining the prayer call I have become more diligent in my quest to open my second business and grow the existing business. Taking lessons from "Dare to Walk in My Shoes" by Nicole Jones, "The Dynamic Laws of Prosperity" by Catherine Ponder and "Speak it Into Existence by Sesvalah, I am practicing great spiritual rituals that are the foundation of a prosperous life. Who would have imagined that I would experience such joy while doing so? Don't get me wrong, I still have to pray about remaining positive in word, thought and deeds, but my walk is becoming an innate part of my being every day. I feel happier, I get up and go every morning with the Lord on my side and, hence, I am more aware of my spiritual center to radiate the same back.

I am a child of God and so are my children. I want and will receive blessings of overflow and abundance; however, I am learning to eliminate the conscious thought of "hurry" (immediate results) because you cannot rush God. I may be in a situation that I am working myself out of financially and emotionally, but I AM WORKING MYSELF OUT and INTO A MORE PROSPEROUS position in life all around. I cannot do anything without God and would not want to try.

This community of prayer warriors I commune with on a daily basis is like my extended family. Even though I don't know every individual, they speak to my heart in a huge manner! If I can get up and take a shower and walk out into the world, I can make God my first and last priority of every day without excuse or exception. I have come to depend on this prayer community. After each lesson I walk daily with the Lord on my mind, with a plan of execution relative to the things I need to do to move to an even higher level. I can't and won't complain about my situation because it is simply a situation and not my position in life. It is only temporary, and it could be worse! I know that my God will not put more on me than I can bear. The Lord helps those who help themselves, however, you must have the faith of a mustard seed.

Don't get me wrong—I do have my days, but I am alive, healthy and have my beautiful children. My faith is challenged constantly especially when it comes to mounting bills and no positive income to show for it. Nonetheless, I'm beginning to heal myself, love myself and radiate that love to others which include forgiveness. In doing so, each day gets lighter.

Each person's walk is different. In order for me to get to the place I want and will be I had to let go of a lot of things, people and reposition my frame of mind and way of thinking. My goal is to attract God-like things and individuals, therefore, I had to change my attitude about myself and others. I affirm and speak everything into existence with clarity, certainty and specificity asking that he continues to wrap his loving wings around my family and I, and continue to walk with me every step of the way.

The Will of God will never take you where the Grace of God cannot keep you, where the Arms of God cannot support you, where the Riches of God cannot support your needs, where the power of God cannot endow you, where the Army of God cannot protect you.

Affirmation: I release all things negative and judgmental. I release hurt, pain, affliction, anger, hostility, vengeance, and inharmonious situations/relationships. I attract and accept the spirit of God, prosperity in overflow and abundance, good health, love, marriage, renewed resources and financial status and harmonious God-centered situations/relationships.

The Lord is my Shepherd I shall not want!!!

With Love and Peace.

From me to you with love, Janine.

Roslyn Joshua

I joined the prayer line in October of 2009. Since I have started the prayer line, my life has changed. I know how to love myself and respect myself and others. I walk differently, I talk differently, I think differently, and I love differently. Every morning we are greeted my Janine's soft voice; a peaceful tone, one that relaxes the spirit. The assignments that she gives us every day have helped me through so many trials. Since I have been journaling, praying and fasting God has done some GREAT things! I prayed for peace on my job with my supervisor, and it is now coming into fruition. I prayed for someone to pay me back and they did. AMEN!!! Since being on the prayer line I have learned to eat right and watch what I put in my body. As a result, I lost ten pounds and counting.

I thank Janine for allowing me to see that I was blocking myself from God's Blessings that He has for me. Janine is such a remarkable person. I thank you for opening my eyes to a new world of peace, love, joy and prosperity.

Tiffany Hill

God has such a way with timing; He's the master of all timepieces. When God brings people together it's a divine union. I connected with Janine in a very important time in my life and my children's life. My children are developing more into their own persons; and I want to plant a good seed in them. I was seeking God for direction, wisdom and understanding on parenting. I was determined to lay a good foundation for my children. It all starts with a good foundation, things will come up but they will not over take you if your foundation is laid with God's words and promises.

When I met Janine's three awesome daughters, (Diamond, Ebony and Asia) I knew instantly—someone had laid a solid foundation and God had blossomed them into young women. That is the exact desire I have for my son and daughter. I wanted to get the formula right; it was a must that I sit down with Janine to hear her testimonies about her parenting skills. I believe with all my heart that God gives us tangible things or people we can relate to, share with, and explore each other's minds. That's exactly what I wanted to do with Janine, to see how she produced such wise young girls. I knew it was the power of God, but I was interested in how Janine released her own thoughts/rules about parenting and totally surrender to God's way. That's the key; you must have an obedient ear to hear what direction God has laid out for you as a parent; that way you are able to minister into your children life. The obedience will allow you to speak things into existence and degree greatness into your children's life.

Obedience is the greatest sacrifice as there is so much victory in obedience. I knew all these things, but yet I was still struggling to really let go and let God. I was stressed about everything that came up in their lives; not the correct way to operate when you know Who You Belong To—the King of kings and Lord of lords. Talking with Janine and sharing my experiences made things better, as I knew God is no respecter of person. I, too, could receive the blessing of parenting through God's holy spirit. God blessed us with these angels but sometimes we get caught up in traditions and what we expect of our children that we miss the most important rule of parenting which is "seeking God." We must seek God, for all answers and if we have an ear to hear Him, God will direct our path. Decree victory over yourself, your family, and friends walk in faith and watch God show up and show out.

I firmly believe …

Death and life are in the power of the tongue: and they that love it shall eat the fruit thereof.
                              Proverbs 18:21 (King James Version)
For I know the plans I have for you," declares the LORD, "plans to prosper you and not to harm you, plans to give you hope and a future.
                              Jeremiah 29:11 (New International Version)

Diamond Ingram

There came a time in my life that I couldn't figure out what my passion was. I knew the sky was the limit, but things did not come as quickly as I would have liked. I had recently graduated from a high ranked university, I had applied and interviewed with major corporations and I had done an awesome internship in Italy for a few months along with several other experiences that made my resume stand out. But I still had no idea what I wanted to do. This was not a good feeling as I had done everything by the books but I was not sure of my next steps.

My mother would always tell my sisters and I write your goals, say your affirmations and visualize what you want. She would remind us that we have to have faith and know that God will work things out. Just enjoy life!

Finally, at 23-years-old, I decided to actually put to practice those things she would tell us and what I would see her do. I figured, what could it hurt at this point? I didn't have a full-time job and the things I was doing did not fulfill me. I spoke to my Mom, told her my thoughts and she told me to start with the basics and simply write down the things that make me happy. I began to put this in practice every day and pray, and things started to become clear each day.

From there I decided to apply to graduate school as well as

apply to a job that I had wanted since graduation. My mother guided me through this process with the creation of my first vision board. Now, I am in a top graduate school making straight A's, and I got the job that I had wanted. She has been my guiding light and she is such a phenomenal and inspiring woman. I love you!

Ebony Ingram

The first word we were all taught to spell was success. Every morning would start with the song "S-U-C-C-E-S-S! THAT IS HOW YOU SPELL SUCCESS!" It was not something we just spelled, it was yelled with exuberance; we gave life to those words every morning. This would be followed by a meditation session lit by a small candle sitting in the center of our prayer circle and the rising sun. Then came the getting dressed part and the very brutal "hair doing session."

Our weeks would be sprinkled with extracurricular activities including piano lessons, saxophone lessons, dance classes, basketball practice, Saturday school and after school programs, which at the time did not seem that time consuming. We stayed active and, as active as we were, my parents always found a way to be involved in those activities. They were constantly motivating and pushing, but never forceful but demanded only our very best.

My sisters and I stayed in competitive activities. We were never taught "I'm better than my competitor," however, we were taught to be better than yesterday's best and to manifest the God within us. Before every competition, game or performance, we were taught a ritual that included prayer, visualization and affirmation. Mom always said "the body reacts positively to positive words," and "if you can see yourself doing it, you can do it." This repeatedly brought about positive outcomes. Any loss never felt like a loss because with positive thoughts and words, we were prepared to pick ourselves up and fight another day.

Though my mother taught us all the same thing, she encouraged individualism within each of us. She has raised a businesswoman, an artist and a scientist. We all have some knowledge in each field, but we all have different focuses. We have chosen to travel upon paths that enhance and highlight our talents. No, we are not perfect and, of course, we have been met with difficulties on these paths. Giving up, however, has never been encouraged in our home. Having a mom with no fear and the most faith makes staying on this path that much easier.

My mother has also taught us that success is not having the most money, but it is truly being satisfied with where you are. To never want for anything, and should I want for anything, I am equipped with the tools to get it. Limits only exist in the mind and the rest is up to me. When I run into a "no," that never means no; it means try again, differently this time.

Honestly, as a freshman at Howard University, I cannot say that I have a clear picture of where I'm going but I can say that I feel positive about my future. Failure and mediocrity is clearly not an option with the tools I have been given. My mother is open and constantly willing to learn new things. As she learns, grows and gains more tools, she selflessly brings them back to us and shares them with the world.

Asia Ingram

In the midst of working hard to become successful in my life, my mom has been the key to my perseverance. Through mental and visual exercises, artistic exercises like vision boards and creating list that amplify my positive attributes, I have become a successful high school senior. When I say successful, I don't just literally mean grades and awards, but I have had a successful transformation of attitude and confidence.

No I'm not perfect, and nowhere close to nearing it, but I have perfected the person I am today. With little steps with the guidance of God and my family, I grow closer to the person I am meant to be.

Recommended Reading List

Dynamic Laws of Prosperity by Catherine Ponder
Millionaire Moses by Catherine Ponder
Millionaire Joshua by Catherine Ponder
Millionaire from Genesis by Catherine Ponder
Millionaire from Nazareth by Catherine Ponder
Speak It into Existence by Sesvalah & Naleighna Kai
    (www.sesvalah.com and www.naleighnakai.com)
Dare to Walk in My Shoes by Nicole Jones
    (www.daretowalkinmyshoes.com)
Think and Grow Rich by Napoleon Hill
Science of Getting Rich by Wallace D Wattles
The Writings of Florence Scovel Shinn the complete
collection

Janine A. Ingram

As a life coach, visionary, inspirational speaker, prayer line facilitator, and community liaison, Janine A. Ingram has dedicated her passion to shaping the social and spiritual awareness of the Inner-City community. Janine's true gift as a leader allows her to embrace spiritual values while combining a thirst for success and hunger for knowledge with an enthusiastic approach to taking on new challenges—all of which catapulted her to the top of the community service industry. In keeping with her mission, her work as an executive director with the Changing Patterns for Families agency, was a reflection of her passion for excellence, and the pledge to provide a positive contribution, and implement innovative ideas that would help transform dreams into reality.

Janine's main objective is encouraging people to become architects of their own lives using building blocks of love, wisdom, faith, and courage. She has always believed that combining faith and Divine right action gives the ability to write the lyrics to our own song; to paint the canvas of our lives based on direction from the inner spirit and God-given talents. Her goals are to educate, motivate, and help elevate the consciousness of everyone she encounters, leaving a trail of successful and inspired people in her wake.

www.janineingram.com
ingram_janine@yahoo.com